Smart Baseball Umpiring

How to Get Better Every Game

by George Demetriou and Bill Topp

Referee Enterprises, Inc.
Franksville, Wis.

Smart Baseball Umpiring — How to get better every game
by George Demetriou and Bill Topp

Cover design by Matt Bowen, *Referee* publication design manager
Book layout by Lisa Martin, *Referee* art & creative director
Edited by Bill Topp, *Referee* senior associate editor

Printed in the United States of America.

ISBN 1-58208-007-0

Table of Contents

Introduction

Anyone who has umpired a while knows outs and safes, balls and strikes are *not* what umpiring is all about. Your presentation and mental approach are equally important when defining the complete umpire.

Smart Baseball Umpiring — How to get better every game gives you some things to think about beyond casebook plays and field diagrams. It offers you a chance to step back from your daily umpiring duties and focus on why you're out there and what you can do to improve each time you go on the field. The book will help you figure out just what it is you need to do to elevate your performance, whether you're trying to climb the ladder to the next level or are just wanting to be the best umpire you can be at the level you're currently working.

Throughout the book, there will be occasional rule references when examining some plays. Please note that all rule reference numbers used in this book are subject to change due to the timing of rulebook publication.

Co-author George Demetriou, a multi-sport official from Colorado Springs, Colo., who is president of the Colorado Baseball Umpires Association provides most of the valuable insight within these pages. He is among the best officiating authors in the country and we are proud to share his thoughts with you.

As with all *Referee* books, you'll likely agree with some of the things we offer and might disagree with some others. We're OK with that. That's how we all learn together. Apply what makes sense to you and other umpires in your area. Let us know how we can make this book better.

Bill Topp
Senior Associate Editor

1

The Mobile Plate Umpire

By George Demetriou

Kevin Keller,
Canyon Country, Calif.

In last season's *Referee* baseball book, *The Umpire's Guide: 1998*, I described six principles of calling balls and strikes. Although that is the heart of working the plate, a good umpire-in-chief does much more than that. A baseball camp I attended several years ago featured Mike and Ray Di Muro, then both Triple-A umpires. Their dad, the late Lou Di Muro, was a top notch AL umpire for many years. About 20 years ago, on a break from the major leagues, Lou attended his son's youth league game in Phoenix and was pressed into service as the plate umpire when the scheduled ump didn't show. Ray recalls being astounded to see his father hustle to third to call a play, an act theretofore unseen in that league. However, he never really understood why his father did that until he became an umpire himself. Coverage of certain plays at third is only one of the myriad responsibilities of the plate umpire.

A good plate arbiter is mobile. In the major leagues, with a four-man crew, you don't see the man behind the dish move very far. In the two-person system, the plate umpire may be required to make a call at each base. You can partially compensate for lack of speed by anticipating the play and getting a quick start to the proper position. In this chapter, I'll help you do that by describing the non-ball and strike duties of the plate umpire in the two-person umpiring system.

FAIR/FOUL

With no runners on base, the base umpire (BU) is on the first base foul line ("A" position). Fair/foul coverage on the first base line is divided. As the plate umpire, you will take any ball which stops short of first base or is touched before reaching the base. Any ball which passes the base (front edge) untouched is BU's responsibility. You must cover the entire third base line. With runners on base, BU is positioned inside the diamond and you have both foul lines in

You must cover the entire third base line.

their entirety.

Surprisingly, there are many umpires who believe any ball which touches the ground before reaching first base is the plate man's responsibility, even if it passes the base. I umpired for many years thinking that and then fell into a false sense of security believing my partners always understood it the way I did — once the ball passes the base it belongs to BU (when he's on the foul line). In a game last year, I had the plate with Bob Kachel on the foul line. A hot smash was drilled down the first base line, bouncing several times before passing about two inches outside the base. Bob leaped into fair territory to avoid the ball and when he didn't immediately make a call, I took it and screamed "foul ball." After the inning was over, I apologized to Bob for being so quick to take his call. His reply: "What do you mean? That *was* your call!" When we brought it up at the next association meeting, we found five more veterans who believed the called belonged to the plate umpire unless it passed first base in flight. The point here is to make this an item in the pregame discussion.

On a ball where fair/foul is a factor, either a ground ball or a fly ball, you must first pause, read the flight of the ball and then react by clearing the catcher, removing your mask (if possible) and setting by straddling the appropriate foul line. The mask should be removed, but on screaming line drives or on bunts which the catcher immediately pounces on, you may not have time. Do not make a call until the play occurs, meaning a ground ball is touched or passes the base or a fly ball lands. If the ball is foul, you should raise your arms, exclaim, "Foul ball," and then point foul with the outside arm. There is no voice on fair balls; merely point to fair territory with the inside arm. The closer the ball is to the foul line, the more emphatic the call. Selling the call is part of umpiring. No signal is needed on obvious fouls (roughly more than 20' foul).

INFIELD GROUNDERS

With no runners on base, for ground balls hit in the infield where fair/foul is not a factor, you should immediately advance up the first base line, striving to get as close to the start of the three foot lane as possible and taking a standing set before the play occurs.

There are three reasons for doing that. You must watch for interference by the batter-runner while out of the three foot lane. You must be ready for overthrows, being prepared to bounce into foul territory and rule on a dead ball and any subsequent award. Finally, from that position you can assist on a pulled foot and/or swipe tag, if asked.

You must be ready for overthrows.

If you're required to make a fair/foul call, advance after making that call (fair balls only). You must clear the catcher to his left or allow the catcher to clear before advancing. A good catcher will break toward the first base dugout to back up an overthrow.

With runners on base, you're responsible for the lead runner if he may attempt to score and thus cannot advance up the first base line. You may also be responsible (depending on the pregame) for the lead runner if he is not put out on the first play. That includes a runner on second who may attempt to advance to third and don't forget a runner on first who once in a while tries to go all the way to third, usually on a bunt.

LINE DRIVES

Line drives caught in the infield above the knee call themselves. When the possibility of a trap exists, one umpire must make the call.

The plate umpire always has line drives to the pitcher. With no runners, BU takes the first baseman and the second baseman coming straight in or to his left. You have the rest. With runners on and BU in either "B" or "C," BU has all line drives except the pitcher and anything caught toward a foul line.

The plate umpire always has line drives to the pitcher.

FLY BALL COVERAGE

With no runners on base, the outfield is divided in half for fly balls (or line drives). BU from his position on the foul line takes anything hit to the center fielder (straight in or straight back) over to the right field foul line if he decides to go out. If BU doesn't go out, responsibility reverts to you. You always have any ball to the center fielder's right over to the left field foul line.

The plate umpire's reaction to a fly ball in his coverage area is influenced by whether the ball is routine or a "trouble" ball. The four criteria for a trouble ball: a ball near a foul line, a hard run in (ball which may be caught below the waist or trapped), dead run out (ball approaches a fence or fielder turns his back to the infield), or two fielders converge towards a possible collision. You must move more aggressively for a trouble ball than for a routine fly.

When the ball is hit, pause, read the position of the fielder making the play and react by determining whether the ball is in your coverage area and whether it is routine or trouble. If routine, move in the general direction of the play and let your partner know the catch is made, "Bill, that's a catch." There is no need to signal.

For a trouble ball, move aggressively as close to the play as possible while striving for the best (90 degree) angle possible to see the catch/no catch. In most cases, moving along the foul line will give the best angle. Moving toward the fielder is generally not a good idea. A possible exception is when fielders are converging.

In most cases, moving along the foul line will give the best angle.

Either sell the catch by signaling and proclaiming it vigorously or sell the no catch by repeatedly giving the safe signal and shouting, "No, no."

With runners on base, BU is positioned inside the diamond and takes anything between the right and left fielders, but should not cross the baseline to go out on any fly ball. You're responsible for anything from the right and left fielders over to their nearest foul line.

TAG UPS

The UIC is always responsible for a runner at third with BU

having first and second. When the ball is hit: pause, read the position of the fielder making the play and the runner's actions, and react by moving toward the third base dugout to get a panoramic view of both catch and tag. Be prepared to get back to the plate if a play develops there (more on that later). You must stay on the line if you have a fair/foul decision to make.

Remember, when in doubt, the runner did not leave the base too soon. Federation rules require the umpire to call the runner out if he has left his base before a fly ball is caught (touched). Pro and NCAA insist on the defense appealing that play. I can recall a runner leaving too soon only once. A brain dead high school kid left third when the ball was 10 feet from the left fielder's glove. My call was easy, but if there is any doubt whatsoever in your mind, the runner did not leave early.

> **When in doubt, the runner did not leave the base too soon.**

PLAYS AT THIRD

There are several situations when you are responsible for covering third; other situations are optional depending on crew preferences. The various mechanics manuals may differ on the optional coverages and you'll see some variety among clinicians. I'll cover the approach recommended by *Referee*.

The play which will bring you to third most often is a base hit to the outfield with a lone runner at first. When the ball is batted: pause, read the position of the fielder and the speed of the runner and react by clearing the catcher and moving up the third baseline in foul territory, about 6-10' from the line. Let your partner know: "Bill I've got third. I've got third." If a play develops, pop into fair territory and make the call from the edge of the notch. You can get there in sufficient time to take a hands on knees set. If you take too long to read the play and don't react immediately, you'll probably be moving when the play occurs, no matter how fast you are. Please note that procedure is an abbreviated version of what is taught in professional umpire schools.

When a time play is possible (two out), you must be certain you know which came first: the score or the out.

With runners on first and third, you can proceed as above and look back to see the lead runner touch the plate. With runners on first and second, you must stay home because of the possibility of a play on the lead runner at the plate. When a time play is possible (two out), you must be certain you know which came first: the score or the out.

In the Colorado Rockies home opener against the St. Louis Cardinals on April 7, 1998, a time play was a factor in the Cards 12-11 victory. In the seventh, the Rockies had runners on the corners with one out. Neifi Perez sent a liner into the right-center gap. Ray Lankford made a lunging grab and fired back to the infield to easily double up Vinny Castilla at first. Rookie Todd Helton had tagged up at third, but not knowing the applicable rule, apparently stopped to yell at Castilla to get back. Plate umpire Jerry Layne ruled the out at first was made before Helton touched the plate and disallowed the run, though replays later showed that Helton crossed the plate before the out. You likely won't have replays to second-guess your every move, but if you recognize a time play and are prepared, you'll get it right.

When a ground ball is hit within the infield, as discussed earlier, there are several situations when the plate umpire may cover third. They include: a lone runner on second who may attempt to advance after the throw to first, a runner on first who may try to take two bases on a bunt, or runners on first and second and a double play is attempted. In the latter case, an ensuing play at third is rare, but make sure both umpires understand who is responsible if it happens.

The pregame discussion with your partner should cover who will be at third for the following situations: no runners and the batter-runner goes for a triple, an overthrow on steal of second (BU preferred), an overthrow on a pickoff at second (BU preferred), a runner at second who tags on a routine fly ball. Please note in the latter case, if you must rule fair/foul on the right field line, BU must take the play at third and you should announce, "I'm staying home" or, "I'm on the line." *Referee* recommendation: UIC covers third on a tag up at second (with the above exception) and on a lone batter-runner going to third. That uses both umpires and maximizes flexibility.

In making the call at third, you should remember that when in doubt, the runner is out when the ball beats him. Many coaches believe if the ball beats the runner, the runner is out, regardless of where the tag is applied. I do not accept that and hope you don't either. Now, when there's *doubt*, I do accept it. On occasion, you may have to make a call from less than the optimum angle. If you don't see the tag and can't tell if the runner gets his foot on the base before the glove is applied, but the ball clearly beats the runner with the fielder getting the glove down, call the out.

> **Many coaches believe if the ball beats the runner, the runner is out, regardless of where the tag is applied.**

BASE TOUCHING

With no runners on base, whenever BU goes out on a fly ball, you are responsible for the batter-runner touching first and second, if necessary. In fact, you won't get any help from BU unless the play ends up at the plate. In that case, BU should return to the plate area in foul ground and be prepared to make the call.

Most of the time, the UIC has base touching responsibility at third. On a base hit with a runner on second, you must get down the line in foul territory to watch the touch at third. The touch will be hard to see clearly because the runner will go for the inside corner while your view is from foul territory, but make sure he comes close. With multiple runners, your primary responsibility is to watch the runner as he scores. In those situations, you won't be able to get as far up the line as when there is only one runner to worry about.

When in doubt, the runner touched the base. Frequently, the umpire will not be close enough to see the actual contact. Don't

When in doubt, the runner touched the base.

worry about it. If the runner's foot was close enough to the base, so that he could have touched it, and you didn't clearly see him miss it, he touched it. The missed base rule is for players who cut corners or miss by a foot.

In Game Five of the 1991 NL Championship Series, umpire Frank Pulli called Atlanta's Dave Justice out on appeal for missing third. Justice was on second and tried to score on a base hit. The replay showed a tuft of dust as Justice's foot passed over the base, but was inconclusive as to whether his cleat ever touched the base. In an amateur game, there should be no debate: If the foot got that close, the runner touched the base.

RUNDOWNS

For rundowns between third and home, the UIC is in a great starting position for his end of the play. The remaining possibilities (between first and second or second and third) are initially the responsibility of BU. You can and should move into position to take either the first or third base end of those plays. With multiple runners, you may end up taking total responsibility for the rundown.

As a rundown play develops, you should approach in foul ground and when you're ready to take your end, you should wait until the ball is going away from you before stepping into position in fair territory. Announce, "George, I've got this end." Only then should BU back off toward second base. If you step in as the play is coming toward you and a tag is immediately made, there is a good chance two umpires will make a call (hopefully the same one).

As UIC in a game a few years ago, I failed to follow my own advice. The batter-runner rounded first on an overthrow, went halfway to second and correctly decided he couldn't make it there. It wasn't much of a rundown because he was immediately chased back to first. I came in as he was returning to first and, without announcing my presence, called him safe while still moving. My partner, relatively inexperienced, did not recognize my faux pas. He had lagged behind the play and was in a poor position to see the tag at first. As I was shouting safe, I looked over to see my partner's arm cocked for the out. Fortunately, no one else noticed and my call was accepted with nary a word.

PLAYS AT THE PLATE

The baseball world is divided on the best position to call a tag play at the plate. There are advocates of both the first base line extended and the third base line extended. First of all, as UIC, you must observe all scoring runners touch the plate (except when you've covered a play at third and the BU covers the plate, as previously reviewed). When a runner is coming in, he is the priority. BU will have to cover whatever else is going on.

> **The baseball world is divided on the best position to call a tag play at the plate.**

As the play develops, it's preferable to stand directly behind the plate until the throw can be read. If the throw is off line and is up either foul line, the best position is the third base line extended. From that position, there is a good view of the standing tag which may be attempted. If the throw is on target and the catcher gets down to block the plate, the first base line extended is better. That position will give the desired 90 degree angle into the slide and tag. In both cases, 10-12' from the play is optimum.

CLEARING THE BAT

With runners coming in, the safety conscious and courteous umpire will get the bat out of harms way, if possible. It may deflect a thrown ball or even worse, inhibit or injure a sliding runner. Never pick up the bat and toss it. More than one on deck batter or preceding runner has been clobbered by a well-meaning umpire. Kicking the bat is also not a good idea; it's difficult to control where it'll go. The

> **Never pick up the bat and toss it.**

recommended technique is to bend over, grasp the middle of the bat and slide it away. That may be worthy of mention in the pregame conference with the coaches. I've had several cases of near interference and at least one case of interference as on deck batters or runners which have scored, have attempted to retrieve the bat.

POP UPS

Pop ups in fair territory to all infield positions are the responsibility of the plate ump; you should come out from the plate no further than halfway to the mound to call them. Pop ups which are obviously foul between home and first base are initially a joint responsibility. Both umpires should go into foul territory, keeping the fielder between them. Whomever the fielder is facing when he catches or misses the ball should make the call. If the catch is made facing neither umpire, the closest umpire is responsible.

When the ball is fouled in the air behind the plate, the first priority is to clear the catcher. To do that, "open the gate" to the catcher's box so he's not impeded. That is similar to BU opening the gate on a steal of second. Most of the time (particularly if you are in a good slot position), the catcher will move away from you. The direction you turn is dependent on the catcher's initial movement. Take a half step back toward the screen with the foot closest to the direction the catcher takes and cross over with the other foot. Take your mask off and keep your eye on the catcher, not the ball. Move with the catcher, keeping at least 10 feet from him. The catcher will take you to the ball. If he doesn't, you don't have a call to make.

A good catcher will hold on to his mask until he has a bead on the ball. You can't afford to worry about where he throws it. On most amateur fields, fan interference is not likely, but if necessary, be aware of the possibility. In most situations, you can keep your eyes on the catcher's glove. That's where the play will or will not be made. The one exception is if the catcher approaches a high screen. In that case you must pick up the ball in flight to ensure it doesn't graze any fencing.

INFIELD FLY

An infield fly can occur with runners on first and second or the bases loaded and less than two out. In such a situation, the umpires should remind each other before the next pitch to the following batter by signaling "pledge of allegiance" - right hand on left breast (generally used in pro) or by pointing to the bill of the cap with the right index finger (generally, NCAA).

The rule states "ordinary effort." In order to determine if the ball can be caught with ordinary effort, you must wait for the ball to reach its apex. If the fielder is camped under the ball when it starts coming down, that's ordinary effort. If he has no clue where it is, you won't call an infield fly. Anything in between is a judgment call (I never promised you all the answers). Some guidelines: Anytime the fielder turns his back to the infield, you probably have more than ordinary effort. If the fielder is looking into the sun or on windy days, wait a little longer than usual before you call it.

> **To determine if the ball can be caught with ordinary effort, you must wait for the ball to reach its apex.**

Please remember the purpose of the rule is to avoid a cheap double play. Assuming the batter-runner runs to first base as he should on all fly balls, the double play would be initiated by a throw to third to force R2 followed by a throw to second to get R1. If the ball drops, the frustrated fielder almost always throws to second for an easy out. My point is that if you don't declare an infield fly in a marginal situation, it's unlikely to cause any harm.

Either umpire can call an infield fly. Most of the time, you will make the initial call; you have the panoramic view and can judge ordinary effort quicker. BU should echo the call: "Infield fly, batter is out." If the ball is near a foul line, the correct

> **Either umpire can call an infield fly.**

call is, "Infield fly, if fair." The proper mechanic is to point to the sky with your index finger and follow with your out signal.

PUTTING BALL IN PLAY

Just about every plate umpire begins the game by announcing, "Play ball." For many umpires, that's only time they formally put the ball in play. The rules require you indicate the ball is live to start each half inning and after each dead ball. Simply point to the pitcher and say, "Play." It alerts everyone an out can be recorded. After a foul ball with no runners on base, the odds are no one will notice if you don't put the ball in play. I do it to keep myself in the game and to let the pitcher know I'm ready. If you're worried about getting hoarse because of a zillion foul balls, pass on the voice and simply point. Forget to do that with base runners (voice is crucial there) and you're courting disaster.

If you frequently pass on "play," it's only a matter of time before the pitcher picks off a runner with a dead ball and your partner bangs the out. You'll then have one coach who will feel cheated and you're the one who has to explain.

If you erroneously put the ball in play, the ball remains dead despite your proclamation. The following play occurred when I was behind the plate at Lewis Palmer High School in Monument, Colo., several years ago. With a runner on third, the safety squeeze rolled foul. The pitcher fielded the ball and with a sleight of hand gave it to the third baseman. I believe everyone in the park except for those two players, thought the pitcher had the ball. The pitcher engaged the rubber and I yelled "play" whereupon the third baseman tagged the surprised runner. The only plausible choices are balk or no play. The official ruling by interpretation is "no play." The ball was improperly declared live. Although I was not aware of the interpretation at the time, I managed to get it right and best of all, got no argument!

CALLING "TIME"

Try to limit calling time if for no other reason than to reduce the instances you have to put the ball back into play. Repeated requests from the same batter should be denied. You don't need to call time to clean the plate, but be careful with a runner on third. Home has been stolen in the major leagues at least once with the man in blue bent over the plate. After you cover a play at third and the runner is out, it's OK to turn your back to infield to return to the plate without calling time. BU can cover the remaining runner. If the runner is safe, don't turn your back and leave your partner with two runners; that's a good time to kill the ball.

Repeated requests from the same batter should be denied.

CLEANING THE PLATE

I'll close with a housekeeping tidbit. Yes, there is a right way and a wrong way to brush the dirt off the dish. The underlying principle: Never moon the spectators. Turn your back to the pitcher's rubber and use firm strokes. Start each half inning with a totally clean plate; it'll reduce the need to clean it while a batter is in the box. I limit my scrubs to between batters or conferences unless I get a request. If the catcher takes it upon himself to use his glove as a broom, I cheerfully interject, "I'll do that for you."

2

Analyzing Your Performance

By George Demetriou

Tom Thompson, Simi Valley, Calif.

You're only as good as your next game. It doesn't matter if you've put together several seasons of perfect games. When you go on the field for the next game, the players and coaches care only how you do in that game.

I never really thought about the irrelevance of past games until a couple of seasons ago. Ross MacAskill, a 24-year veteran, and I were partners for a March 1997 high school baseball game. It was a spring break tournament in Colorado Springs and our schedule read, "Winner #1 vs. Winner #2." Ross had the plate and while he was getting dressed in the parking lot, I went inside the stadium to check the progress of the previous game. When I returned, Ross asked "Who do we have?" I replied, "Hays, (Kansas) vs. Arvada West (Denver)." Ross chuckled, "So, our reputations mean nothing today!"

Arguably, a good reputation is of value in preventing or defusing confrontations, but in the end, a reputation has never helped any official make the right call. It really didn't matter if we were umpiring for schools we'd never seen and probably wouldn't see again or whether they were local schools we see several times each year.

In order to become a better official, you must recognize you are not perfect and you must have the will to learn. When you get to the point where you know it all, it's probably time to retire. In this chapter, I'm going to outline a technique for self-evaluation.

Almost no one likes evaluations. Evaluation can be a difficult thing to accept because it sometimes hits home in ways which attack one's sense of self and also because it sometimes is so far off the mark it infuriates the recipient. Most people shun the prospect of being evaluated, but performance assessment is done all the time in the real world, whether it is business, academia or social interacting.

In my regular job, I get an annual evaluation. The critique is always the same: "You do great work but you don't document it properly." My reply is memorized: "I'll work on that." I then sign a form indicating I've been counseled and that gets me a pay raise. I'd almost rather not get the raise and not have to sit there and listen.

About 10 years ago, the Southeastern Conference (SEC) conducted a survey of its officials. A top five "likes" and "dislikes" list was published. Travel away from family was the most disliked aspect of SEC officiating and evaluations were right after that. Travel also made the top five "likes" list, but I'll not get into that here.

Judging is going on openly or subtly. We operate in a very public way and we're often gazed at through cruel eyes. We should welcome attempts to look at our efforts dispassionately.

In the early 1980s, I was the operations officer for a field artillery battalion in Germany. We spent most of our time training for various types of combat missions. Our division artillery commander (next higher level) emphasized evaluations. He rightfully believed that to get the most out of training, you had to get meaningful feedback. Consequently, all training exercises had to have evaluation plans. One day the division artillery operations officer engaged me in an impromptu discussion on an upcoming training exercise. He asked about my evaluation plan and I replied, "Why does everything need to be evaluated?" He threw me out of his office.

The problem with evaluating everything was limited resources. Splitting your people into trainees and evaluators precludes realistic training because the full complement of personnel was not available. Trading off with other units to evaluate each other has its merits, but doubles the time required. Besides while senior people were out evaluating, the rest of the personnel went unsupervised and able to perform only limited activities.

Sound like a military problem? Not hardly. Substitute "umpiring crew" for "artillery unit" and it's the same situation. Outside observers can be used to provide feedback. All college conferences and some high school associations have officials supervisors who routinely observe games and provide formal evaluations. These evaluations are generally frank, valid, assessments devoid of politics. However, just like in the military, it's a limited capability. One supervisor can only be at one game at a time.

Additionally, when only one person is in charge, there is a tendency to "grow" everyone with personal idiosyncrasies. Those may not necessarily be the best way to do things. During a recent camp I attended, three different evaluators had three different reactions to the way I respond to the plate umpire's appeal for a checked swing. The first thought I was sharp and professional; the second said I was robotic and mechanical; the third was ambivalent.

Many associations set up their own evaluation system. My high school association uses idle members to observe games and provide feedback. That approach has some value, but as in the military, is very limited. On most days, if a member is available, he's usually needed to work a game.

An often short-changed item is the postgame review. Just as the pregame discussion increases the probability of efficient performance, a postgame review can help you learn from the experience and improve performance the next time. What was done right should receive as much emphasis as areas for improvement.

Evaluation goes on all the time whether we like it or not. Because it is inevitable, it is a sound idea to make it work for you. In the late 1980s, Dr. Roy Askins of Placentia, Calif., offered a set of questions you can ask yourself either periodically or after each game. Once the game is over, you can and should go over what happened and determine why. Be your harshest critic and learn from any errors. Learning from one mistake can help avoid making further mistakes at more critical times. I've built on Askins' work and offer you the following:

PERIODIC REVIEW

The following questions are not necessarily game specific (though they can be) and can be asked several times each season.

Am I open minded?

Arrogance, apathy and complacency are sometimes roadblocks to improvement. It's important you recognize the ways they can manifest themselves in your life and prevent you from keeping an open mind.

Arrogance is a sense of superiority and isn't always a terrible thing. People who are successful have a high regard for themselves. Everyone has an ego and the opposite is low self-esteem, another type of problem. An expansion of the definition of arrogance is, "the offensive display of the feeling of superiority." It is that which creates the greater problem. Arrogant people won't listen to new ideas and their know-it-all attitude can cause errors.

Arrogance is probably the most prominent bad attitude an official can exhibit and it can take numerous forms. An official who acts in a superior manner with his partners will probably act dictatorially with coaches and players. In addition to arrogant officials not listening to fellow officials, they may turn a deaf ear to player complaints or even bark back at coaches when questioned.

You may also see haughty officials ordering around anyone in sight, ground crew, scorekeepers, etc. An arrogant person is likely to demand special favors: "Get me a band aid, will you?" "I'd like a tape job from the trainer." "Gimme two hot dogs between games." Another manifestation of arrogance is accepting only "plum" games and treating other games as beneath consideration or worthy only of cavalier effort. These obtuse individuals often refuse to review any aspect of a game. In short, their minds are closed; their way is the only way and no other way is worth considering.

Apathy is lack of interest or concern. You can easily spot the apathetic official. He shows up just before game time and leaves as soon as it is over. Any mistakes are shrugged off with, "Well, it didn't affect the game."

Another form of apathy is lack of motivation. Most officials start off with lots of desire and commitment, but many find it difficult to maintain a high level of motivation game in and game out through out their career. Even professional officials think about quitting and some do, much earlier than they ever imagined.

Complacency is a smug satisfaction with an existing situation. This disease can strike for short periods or it can be terminal. Veteran officials are the most susceptible. It will strike whenever you neglect preparation, dedication and concentration.

Perhaps the most dangerous form of complacency is allowing your physical condition to deteriorate — it could be life threatening. While baseball is surpassed at least by basketball and soccer for the demand on officials, you can't be credible with the couch potato physique or stamina. Good physical condition will help you stay in the game mentally as well.

A sure sign of a closed mind is when someone brings up a possible new technique. Is your first reaction to reject it out of hand? "If it were any good, someone would have thought of it long ago or it'd be in the book." With that approach, nothing ever changes and initiative is stifled.

If you want to determine if someone has an open mind, engage them in a conversation on which umpire covers third on a triple with no runners for a two-person crew. There are disadvantages either way. If the base umpire is responsible for third, the runner may go halfway to third and change his mind, leaving the umpire in a poor position if the ball is thrown behind the runner to second. Having the plate umpire come up to third brackets the runner, but leaves the plate uncovered should there be an overthrow at third. Those with closed minds will probably insist their method is the only way.

When working with unfamiliar partners, ask and see how

they do things. If they have a different approach, assuming it's proper and doesn't impact teamwork, let them do it in the manner they are accustomed. People do things best when they're allowed the freedom to do it their way. Some examples: How the base umpire asks for help on a possible pulled foot or swipe tag and which umpire makes the call, whether the base umpire stands in the "B" or "C" position with runners on first and third or third base only and how deep he stands in those positions.

Am I ignoring criticism?

It is very easy to dismiss criticism of your work. You may view it as biased, irrational or coming from an inexperienced or uninformed source and you may very well be right. All comments must be put in perspective. It can be helpful to understand why certain criticisms are made by certain audiences at certain times. For example, a coach may complain about close pitches only when he is losing.

The financial and social rewards for officiating are limited. You'll get a lot more criticism than compliments. Some should be heeded, but you cannot get overly concerned about how others view or evaluate your performance.

If there is doubt about the value of a comment you receive, ask a third party. Solicit other opinions. There is more than one valid way to perform many facets of officiating such as exact positioning, going out on fly balls, etc. On occasion, you may receive feedback on something you did correctly, but the discussion may yield a better way of doing it the next time.

As the base umpire with no runners on base, I was in the "A" position. A pop-up was hit down the first base line right at my position. I back pedaled to get out of the fielder's way and to keep my view of the foul line. That necessitated my partner coming up to cover second in the event the ball was fair and the batter-runner attempted to advance to that base. He didn't do it. Our evaluator pointed out I was right and my partner was wrong. The evaluator also pointed out that I could have chosen to pivot with the runner and left the fair/foul decision to the plate umpire. We discussed it and decided the latter method was preferable and that's how we do it now.

Am I overly defensive?

Last season I performed an informal evaluation. On a fly ball to right field, the outfielder caught the ball on the run, but it fell out of his glove as he started to reach for the ball with his throwing hand. The base umpire cocked his arm as if to call the out and then changed to the no catch signal.

During the review, I began with, "Let's talk about the dropped ball in the third inning." The umpire immediately exclaimed, "There was no doubt about that. He dropped that ball before he went to throw it and never had control." He anticipated a criticism he was not going to receive. The issue was not whether he had called the play correctly (he did), but whether he was using proper timing and selling the changed call. His reaction made it virtually impossible to hold a meaningful discussion on either timing or selling calls.

POSTGAME REVIEW

Earlier I mentioned that it was a good idea to evaluate your performance relatively soon after a game. That doesn't mean right after the game. It's better to take some time to unwind, both physically and mentally, after a contest. The next day is probably the ideal time for a review. Here are the questions you can ask yourself after each game.

Did I blow any calls?

The only umpires who haven't blown a call are those who umpire from the stands. To err is human and we probably make more mistakes than we'd like to admit. Sometimes the error, such as an incorrect base award, is subtle and no one (except perhaps your partner) recognizes it. Other times, the mistake (e.g., a call or non-call on interference/obstruction) is out there for all to see and your first thought is to crawl into a hole. The blown call is often the most visible mistake you can make and that is why it is the first item on my postgame list.

Did I make any correct calls for the wrong reason?

Talk about hitting home! No evaluator, except you, will ever pick up on that. How many times did you pass a test in school because you guessed at the answers to a true/false or multiple choice question? On the field, you can guess. You may not understand the situation and get it right out of ignorance or you may be the beneficiary of blind luck.

A common myth in baseball is that on an overthrow, the runner is entitled to the base he is approaching plus one (one plus one). That belief is a carryover from softball. When a thrown ball goes into dead ball territory, the base award can either be one or two bases. If an umpire believes the rule is one plus one in a situation dictating a two base award, he will come up with the right answer for the wrong reason. Here's a play which demonstrates that point along with a variation which causes the wrong rationale to yield a wrong answer.

With one out and a runner on second, the batter hits a deep fly to right. The right fielder catches the ball and his throw to third goes into dead-ball territory. At the time of the throw, R2 is: (a) heading to third after tagging up, or (b) returning to second in order to tag up. In (a), the one plus one philosophy yields the right answer. R2 was heading to third (one base), so he gets one more base, home. In (b), R2 was heading to second (one base), so one more base would put him on third. The correct answer is a two-base award from the base occupied at the time of the throw, so in both (a) and (b), R2 is awarded home. The direction the runner is heading has absolutely no influence on the award.

It's OK to be thankful, but don't count on it next time. If you're sincerely interested in improving your work, you need to find out why the wrong rationale yielded the right answer and how to apply the correct logic. Review the variations so when something like that happens again, you can be confident in your ability to figure it out.

Was there a call I didn't have to make that I would have gotten wrong?

This is another one that only you will ever know about. "Dodging a bullet" is what I call it. The lessons here are just as good as if you had made the mistake, but without the guilt or agony. It may be something that was your partner's call or perhaps a rules situation you didn't have to deal with because you weren't the umpire-in-chief that day. How about "what ifs," variations of actual situations, you may have had difficulty with. Reliving all those and researching the correct answer will help you improve and the best part is no one else has to know.

Here's a situation which more than one umpire has avoided making a mistake. Runner on first breaks as the 3-2 pitch is delivered with two out. As the umpire calls "strike three," the batter interferes with the catcher's throw to second. Since the inning ends on the strike out, the plate umpire does not have to declare the interference and better yet, he doesn't have to enforce any penalty. If you'll recall, the penalty on that type of batter interference is to declare the batter out and return all runners to the base occupied at the time of the pitch. If the batter interferes after striking out, the runner attempting to steal is also out.

Did I uphold, defend or rationalize any improper rulings?

Many officials believe changing a decision is a sign of weakness and will provoke criticism and undermine credibility. In baseball, more so than in most sports, there is a certain amount of truth to that. For example, many believe you cannot reverse a safe/out call because you called it too quick or by going to your partner because he may have had a better angle.

Our purpose on the field is to call them right. If you can't handle criticism (sometimes you'll deserve it) or are overly concerned with an untarnished image, then perhaps umpiring is not for you. If you do make a mistake, you should accept responsibility for it and, if permissible, not victimize the participants by insisting on its correctness. In the long run, inflexibility does more damage to your credibility than anything else.

Did I make any calls that did not reflect what I saw or thought?

That occurs more often than most of us would like to admit. Making calls too quickly (poor timing is one cause) is a common fault.

Timing is a delicate art. You must render your decision without hesitation, but making snap calls will get you in trouble. Several things can happen after the apparent end of a play.

A catch is "the act of a fielder getting secure possession in his hand or glove of a ball in flight and firmly holding it..." It is not a catch if immediately following contact with the ball, the fielder drops it as a result of a collision with another player, a wall or the ground. The critical element is time — complete control of the ball long enough. How much "time" is not defined in any rulebook. I offer the thought that the required time necessary to judge a catch varies depending on the nature of the play.

On a routine catch, when the fielder returns the glove to his body, that is long enough. On a diving shoestring catch, when the fielder raises his glove off the ground to "sell" the catch, that is long enough. Whatever the play, look to see if the fielder has control of what he's doing. If the player has control of his body, it's an indicator that the play is over. In order to make one correct call on a catch, you must wait to see the whole play.

Consistent timing is essential for a plate umpire as well, helping to establish a rhythm. You must have a routine for getting into position, calling the pitch and coming out of position. Relaxing between pitches is part of the routine.

Strive for the balance point in getting into position. If you get set too soon, you will tire faster. Getting set too late will contribute to missing pitches because your head will be moving while the pitch is en route. The professional umpire schools teach a mantra: "On the rubber, get set, call it."
In both cases — balls and strikes — suppress the natural tendency to react immediately. Use your eyes properly to ensure the pitch is completely over before you call it. You can easily spot the rookies who call the pitch before it is caught. Slow timing is better than fast timing, but that doesn't mean you can take forever. If you get into the habit of a slight delay, you can use the additional time to think about what you just saw. Since it's a routine, no one knows you're taking the extra time. On 3-2 pitches with a runner moving, you need to be a tad quicker.

Other causes of improper calls include: making calls on the basis of what is assumed to have happened because of doubt, playing to the crowd and taking the path of least resistance. The guideline is, "call 'em the way you see 'em." You have to work at it to do it.

Was I vulnerable to outside influences?

This is closely related to the previous item. Officiating relies heavily on subjective judgment, thus we all go through cycles where our confidence waxes and wanes. You must be able to admit to yourself that you're vulnerable in certain situations and take the necessary steps to keep from succumbing.

A few years ago I worked the plate in what turned out to be a close game. The visiting coach was a gentleman and had not griped at all the entire game. In the last inning, I called a close pitch on one of his batters a strike. The coach from the third base box, calmly said, "Don't change your zone now." I found myself thinking, "Had I called that pitch different earlier?" "Did he really detect an inconsistency or was he 'working' me?" If he had been a blowhard, I would have easily dismissed his comment. His pleasant tone and previous behavior had created an aura of credibility and I succumbed — he had gotten me thinking.

You must forget the fans. The price of admission includes the right to heckle the umpire. Last year we had a local umpire admit to purposely calling close pitches against the team of the fans who were riding him. No tears were shed when he retired. As long as spectators don't interfere with the game, they should be ignored.

Did I control the game properly?

This is an often ignored aspect of an official's job. In order to have control, you must be in control of yourself. Keep your emotions in check. If you find yourself starting to shout, it's an indication you're starting to lose control. In most games you don't have to do anything; the players control themselves. On occasion you must control the behavior of players, coaches or fans so that the game can proceed in an orderly fashion.

Bench jockeying or the "ragging" of the opponent is a baseball tradition I'd just as soon have forgotten. When it starts, deal with it immediately before it can escalate. Warn players tactfully or have a chat with the coach, "Do you want to deal with them or would you prefer for me to do so?"

Was there a different philosophy that would have resulted in a better outcome?

Officials have more latitude in calling a game than casual observers realize. The size and shape of the strike zone varies from one umpire to another; pick any 10 umpires and you'll find 10 different zones. That power is arbitrary and can strongly influence or determine the outcome of a game, thus it must be applied with great care and in a consistent manner. You must choose an approach that is most likely to be fair to both teams and will reflect the relative merit of play.

A local umpire with professional experience going back to the '60s is known for his very small "pro" strike zone. He prides himself in the consistency of his calls and is admired by many. He is also blackballed by several smaller schools which simply don't have the players to pitch effectively with such a small strike zone.

There is a fine line here. Officials have a responsibility to enforce the rules in a consistent manner, but are not authorized to go onto the field and create new rules or choose which rules to enforce. Examples of rules viewed with disdain are the Federation requirement for the umpire to call out, without appeal, a runner who misses a base or leaves early on a tag; the batter's box rule (Federation and NCAA only), the 20-second delay rule for the pitcher and the requirement for coaches/players to stay in the dugout. You cannot and should not go onto a field and not enforce a rule because you think it's "nit-picking."

On occasion a "no-call" may be appropriate. A no-call is a conscious decision on the part of an official to ignore an infraction. Originally a basketball philosophy, the no-call has limited utility in baseball. Some examples: the "phantom tag" at second where on a double play, the throw is accurate and the pivot man could have tagged second, but in his haste to get out of the way of flying spikes, he cheats a little and kicks the bag before he has the ball or on a slide play without a force, the ball beats the runner and a routine tag could have been made, but the tag is unnecessarily high, or on a routine ground ball, the throw to first is accurate and in plenty of time, but the first baseman pulls his foot a tad quickly. In those cases, the prudent approach is to bang the out. Those are the baseball version of the no-call.

Did I avoid or usurp responsibility at the expense of a partner?

There are occasions when a crew member has to look bad in order to get the play right. Those are rare occasions. Any action which reflects poorly upon a partner should only be taken as a last resort and always in the interest of the game rather than any personal motive.

Here's an example where one umpire goofed, had an opportunity to bail himself out by deferring a call to his partner and chose not to do so. Coverage at third was discussed during the pregame chat and it was agreed that the plate umpire would cover third if a runner on second tried to advance after the throw to first on an infield grounder.

In the second inning such a play occurred, but the plate man lingered to watch the play at first and was horrified to see the runner from second make a run for third. He managed to get a good angle, but was only a third of the way up the line when the tag was made. The base umpire recognized third base was not covered, but didn't have time to get a good angle. The plate umpire's choice: Take the call knowing he'd be blistered for being so far from the play or let his partner take the call. The plate man called the runner "safe" and was immediately greeted by the defensive coach. The umpire preempted the conversation by stating, "The runner got his foot on the back of the bag before the tag was made." The coach replied, "I'm not here for that. I'm here because you're not hustling. How can you make a call like that from this far away?" Had the plate umpire deferred the call, he would have been unscathed, but the wrong call may have resulted because his partner was not in a good position.

Am I a team player?

The previous item contains one example of how umpires can be team players. Let's take it one step further. To move to the highest plateau of umpiring, partners must work and act as a team. Finger pointing as to who had the call on a certain play must be avoided.

In a 1998 game, there was a runner on second with one out. A line drive was hit to the second baseman who trapped the ball. Neither umpire said anything. The fielder immediately threw to first to retire the batter-runner, but his coach declared a catch and got the base umpire (who hadn't watched the play) to declare the double play on the runner. The defense had left the field and when the truth became known, had to return. Both umpires were tarnished over that play, but the worse part was the umpires engaged in an open debate, within ear shot of the coaches, as to who was responsible for the call.

A visible sign of the degree of sophistication of a crew is the way they cover for another in unusual circumstances. Here's another 1998 play: With no runners, a hard grounder was drilled down the first base line bouncing several times before passing just barely outside the base. The base umpire jumped to avoid the ball and when he didn't immediately make a call his partner took it and sold the "foul ball." Had the plate umpire not done that, both umpires probably would have looked bad because the delay in making the call would be interpreted as the umpires not knowing whether the ball was fair or foul. Worse yet, without the foul call, it could have been understood to be a fair ball and the umpires would have been forced to "undo" the play and return runners to get it right.

Do I deal with others appropriately?

A good official is approachable. Reasonable questions should be politely answered. When an unusual play occurs, take the time to explain the outcome to both coaches.

Tact is necessary in dealing with both coaches and players as well as fellow officials. You must have poise at all times and you can't afford to get mad. During arguments, you must be patient and slow to anger. Once you lose your head, you have lost, despite the fact you'll "win" the argument.

Exercising control should be distinguished from exerting power. Power is ego-centered, personalized and confrontational. If you don't take yourself seriously, you won't have trouble avoiding coming across as a power broker.

In a 1994 game in Alamosa, Colo., the out of town coach made one or two comments about low pitches which were called strikes on his batters. On the third comment, the plate umpire ripped off his mask, charged to the third base coaches box and yelled at the coach to knock it off. The umpire was moving so fast, he bumped the coach as he stopped. Afterwards the umpire denied running to the coach's box. The point is not whether he ran, walked fast or crawled, but rather that he appeared to be the aggressor, having gone to the coach. The contact is totally inexcusable. Yes, the umpire was successful in silencing the coach.

Did any of my signals, gestures or my style evoke an unexpected or unwanted response?

Arms folded on the chest is generally recognized as a sign of boredom and many umpire associations prohibit their members from putting their hands in their pockets while on the field. Those are relatively minor gestures and are unlikely to provoke an unwanted response, but here are some tips: Use your palm to say "stop," instead of pointing. Pointing is accusatory. Secondly, don't threaten. If you draw the line at "one more word" and the reply is "OK," are you going to eject?

Many coaches weigh heavily an umpire's attitude toward confrontations and how he handles controversial situations. In Colorado Springs, the number one reason cited by coaches for blackballing umpires is they are unapproachable or curt when they are approached.

Last season, an umpire was reprimanded because of the manner in which he treated an ejected coach. In a prep game during the first week of the season, several balks were called because of the home team pitcher's failure to come to a stop with the entire glove below his chin (a 1998 Federation rule change). After the third balk in the same half-inning, the pitcher indicated frustration so an assistant coach came out to talk to the umpire. The coach's issue was not the balks themselves, but the manner and tone which the umpire had addressed the pitcher. Apparently the umpire had shaken his finger at the pitcher and spoken to him sarcastically. In ejecting the coach, the umpire said "You're gone, good bye, see ya' later" and then followed up by saying goodbye in several different languages.

Although the ejection was upheld by the state association, the umpire's conduct became the larger issue and he was put on probation for "inappropriate, insensitive and offensive" comments.

What can I work on in my next game?

We all have something upon which we can improve. If you're honest with yourself, the previous questions may have identified shortcomings in your work and/or situations which may be troublesome to you. Knowing your shortfalls is the only the first step. Next, we have to resolve to do better.

One technique is to set goals. Edwin Locke, a top researcher in the area of goal setting, defines a goal as attaining a specific standard of proficiency on a task, usually within a specific time limit. Some goals you may consider: getting in a better position to make certain calls, being more decisive or emphatic, keeping calm under pressure, or giving better explanations in tricky situations.

You should identify your goals both for the short term (the next game) and a long term (perhaps the end of the season). Your goals must be challenging, yet realistic. You may find it helpful to write the goal down and think about your strategy for achieving it.

An example of a short-term goal is to make the proper pivot on every pickoff throw. A season goal might be to lower the top end of your strike zone.

Evaluating yourself will make you a better official. Be hard, rake yourself over the coals and then don't forget to forgive yourself.

3

30 Ways to Balk

by George Demetriou

Charles Williams, Engelwood, Calif.

I'll probably retire from umpiring never believing I've seen every possible balk. In terms of specific rules violations there are roughly 30 ways to balk, but when you consider the specific illegal acts which may occur, there are many, many more.

The term "balk" can be traced back to Alexander Cartwright's 1845 rules. Originally, a balk was a pitch which was not delivered underhanded. That later became known as "foul balk" and other acts which were violations of the pitching rule were simply called "balks." By 1884, restrictions on the pitcher's arm movement had been eliminated and the foul balk disappeared. The most recent major revisions to balk rules were made in 1950.

In this chapter, I am going to take you through the subtle world of balks and give practical advice on when to overlook, when to warn and when to call them. Except where noted, the material applies equally to Federation, NCAA and pro rules. *(Editor's note: Rule reference numbers are subject to change.)*

A balk is an illegal act by the pitcher with a runner or runners on base. If it is enforced (more on that later), it entitles all runners to advance one base (pro: 5.09c, NCAA: 9-3 Pen., Fed.: 2-3-1).

Illegal Pitch

A close cousin of the balk is the illegal pitch which is an illegal act with no runners on base. When there is an illegal pitch, the batter is awarded a ball. In pro and NCAA, there are only two acts which are illegal pitches:

1. Pivot foot not in contact with rubber.

2. Quick pitch i.e., before the batter is reasonably set.

Under Federation rules, there are two additional acts which are illegal pitches:

3. Any other violation of the pitching rules.

4. A fielder other than the catcher is in foul ground during delivery (1-1-3).

Also, in Federation rules only, the ball is immediately dead when an illegal pitch is made. Under the other two codes, it is not immediately dead and play proceeds. The following may occur:

- If the batter reaches first in any manner, the illegal pitch is ignored and play proceeds. There are no options.

- If the preceding does not occur, the ball is dead and a ball is awarded to the batter.

Balk penalty

With runners on base, the acts which are illegal pitches result in a balk. Again in Federation, the ball is immediately dead when any balk occurs. In pro and NCAA, the ball remains live after a balk until playing action has ended. When a pitcher balks, the following may occur:

- The pitcher stops, retaining possession of the ball. Result: The ball is dead and all runners are awarded one base. Any count on the batter remains the same.

- The pitcher continues and throws to a base. If the ball is caught, the ball is dead and any out is voided (see above). If the ball is overthrown, runners may advance beyond the base to which they are entitled at their own risk. If all runners do not advance one base, the ball is dead and the balk penalty is enforced.

- The pitcher continues and delivers to the batter. If the batter reaches first in any manner and all other runners advance at least one base, the balk is ignored and play proceeds. If the preceding does not occur, the ball is dead and the balk penalty is enforced (see first item above). There are no options.

Please note a runner who misses the first base to which he is advancing and who is subsequently called out on appeal, is considered to have advanced one base for the purpose of this rule (pro: 8.05 AR 2, NCAA: 8-3n-3 AR 3).

Now, let's review the prohibited acts which result in a balk. First, a definition: The pivot foot is the foot which is in contact with rubber, i.e., the right foot for a right-handed pitcher. Next, there are two pitching positions, the windup and the set. Either can be used at any time. The position is determined by the placement of the pitcher's feet.

For the windup, the non-pivot or free foot must be on or behind the front edge of rubber in Federation (6-1-2); behind the back edge of the rubber in pro (8.01a Comment) and wherever the pitcher wants it to be in NCAA (9-1a). In Federation and pro, if the non-pivot foot is too far forward with respect to the above rule, it is technically a set position. The pitcher must maintain contact with the rubber during delivery. If he drops the heel of his non-pivot foot, it is considered the start of the delivery. The hands may either be together or apart. He may also assume an initial position with the hands apart and then bring them together in a preliminary motion. That is allowed under Pro and NCAA rules, but is technically a balk in Federation (many umpires ignore that infraction).

The set position is characterized by the entire pivot foot in contact with the rubber; some allowance should be made. Professional umpires are generally taught to allow half the foot (heel) to be off the edge of the rubber. If the pitcher's foot is too far off the side of the rubber, have it corrected. To do that, use the catcher or another fielder as the messenger. If you speak directly to the pitcher, you leave yourself open to the opposing coach coming out and advising you the rules do not provide for balk warnings. The rule is intended to restrict the angle at which the ball approaches the plate and a few inches yields no advantage. If the mound is in particularly bad shape, you need to be even more lenient.

The non-pivot foot is to be entirely in front of a line through the front edge of the rubber. The pitcher's stance may be open, (non-pivot foot pointing more to first than home) and he may close it when he comes to a stop. The pitching hand can be at his side or behind his back (more on that later). The hands cannot be together in the initial position. If he engages the rubber with his hands together, he has balked, but I suggest at least one warning before calling it in most situations.

In practicality, the position is indicated by the way the pitcher faces. If he is square to the plate, he is in the windup. If a line through his shoulders is nearly perpendicular to the front edge of the plate (standing sideways), he is in the set position. I've divided balks into four categories: those which can be committed while the pitcher is off the rubber, those which are peculiar to either the windup or the set position and those which can be committed from either position.

OFF RUBBER

Generally, when the pitcher is off the rubber, he has the status of an infielder and most pitching restrictions are not in effect. The pitcher can balk while off the rubber if he attempts to deceive a runner by making any motion naturally associated with pitching.

TAKING SIGNS

All three codes require the pitcher to take the sign while on the rubber, but the penalty differs. The purpose of the rule is to prevent the pitcher from "running the pitch" — quickly engaging the rubber and pitching. If the pitcher takes the sign while off the rubber and there are no runners, a ball is awarded to the batter under Federation (6-1-1 Pen) and NCAA (7-5d) rules. With runners, a ball is also called in NCAA games and it is a balk under Federation rules. In pro (8.01), in all situations a warning is given with possible ejection for subsequent violations.

Hidden ball

You'll see the hidden ball trick at least once a season and it is a legitimate play provided the pitcher does not illegally trick the runner into believing the ball is in the pitcher's glove. The pitcher cannot stand on or astride rubber without the ball (pro: 8.05i). Additionally, in Federation he cannot be within five feet of the rubber (6-2-5) and in NCAA, cannot be on any part of the dirt area of the mound (9-3f). Call a balk in all cases.

Wiping off

The pitcher may touch his pitching hand to his mouth as long as he wipes off that hand before he touches the ball. In Federation and NCAA he may be on the mound, but not on the rubber when he does that. In pro, he must be outside the dirt area of the mound. The penalty for violating either edict differs: Federation: a balk with runners and a ball otherwise; NCAA and Pro: a ball (Pro: 8.02a-1, NCAA: 9-2d, Fed: 6-2-1e).

Delay of game

With the bases empty, the pitcher must pitch, make a play or legal feint within 20 seconds of receiving the ball. The penalty is a ball (pro: 8.04; NCAA: 7-5e, 9-2c; Fed: 6-2-2c). Under Federation rules only, the 20-second limitation also applies with runners on base. Additionally if the pitcher unnecessarily delays the game, a balk can be called in either pro (8.05h) or NCAA (9-3e). In Federation, the pitcher is warned and may be ejected (6-2-2a).

WINDUP POSITION

From the windup position, the pitcher may deliver to the plate or he can step off by first disengaging the rubber with his pivot foot. Under pro and NCAA rules, he may also attempt to pickoff a runner by stepping directly toward an occupied base. Pickoffs from the windup are a balk in Federation; the pitcher cannot feint or throw to any base without first stepping off the rubber.

Once the delivery is started, the motion must be continuous. Under NCAA and Federation rules, he is limited to two pumps or rotations. There is no limit under pro rules.

Step to side

The pitcher may step forward with the non-pivot foot or step backward and then forward. Under pro rules, either step must be directly in front of or behind the rubber; he cannot step to either side. That restriction doesn't exist under NCAA or Federation rules. Literal interpretation of the pro rule would mean the free foot could not be placed outside of a line through the first base edge of the rubber (right-handed pitcher); however, in practice, most umpires allow the pitcher to step outside that line as long as the foot moves more rearward or forward than toward a base. That still allows the runner to determine whether the movement is the start of a delivery or a pickoff attempt. Under Federation rules, it's academic because the pitcher cannot pickoff from the wind-up. The rule doesn't exist in NCAA play.

Contact

Additionally, the rules require the pitcher's entire foot to be in contact with the rubber during the entire delivery. When you're in doubt, the pitcher has sufficient contact. Wait for somebody to gripe before you deal with it.

Dropping heel

Some pitchers will assume the windup position with only the toe of their free foot touching the ground. Their habitual pitching motion begins with the dropping of the heel. If they drop that heel and move the pivot foot to disengage the rubber, it is a balk.

SET POSITION

From the set position, the pitcher may deliver to the plate, he can step off by first disengaging the rubber with his pivot foot or he may also attempt to pickoff a runner by stepping directly toward an occupied base.

Hands

When assuming the set position, Federation and NCAA require the pitching hand to be at the pitcher's side or back. The pro requirement is for either hand to be at his side. Several years ago, a prep league championship in Colorado was decided when the eventual winning run was balked to second in the last inning because the pitcher put his hand "in front of his body." I wasn't there to see it, but apparently the pitcher had done it most of the game without as much as a warning. The umpire who called it hasn't been invited back. The purpose of the rule is to allow the runner to see when the pitcher's hand movement begins. When in doubt as to where the pitcher's hand is, don't worry about it as long as the runner can see part of it.

Starting with the hands apart, the pitcher must bring them together and stop. That is known as the "stretch" and he can only stretch once. In other words, he can't stop twice — stretch and then re-stretch. Once the hands are broken from the stop, the pitcher must either deliver or pickoff; it is a balk if he steps off the rubber. On occasion, a pitcher may come to the stop and discover his stance is too wide. Although the hands don't move, the shortening of the stance is a balk.

Disengaging the rubber

A pitcher may attempt a pickoff as an infielder by first stepping off the rubber backwards. To do that legally, he must move his pivot foot first and it must touch the ground before the hands are separated. Many pitchers move their hands and foot simultaneously. When you're in doubt, the move is legal. Of course, when the pitcher breaks his hands and then moves the foot as an afterthought, you will call the balk (pro: 8.01a Comment; NCAA: 9-1a-1c, 9-1b; Fed: 6.2.4e).

The stop

All three codes require the pitcher to come to a stop in the set position before delivering a pitch. Pro and Federation wording are very close. Pro requires a complete stop and Federation, a complete and discernible stop. That means a Federation stop has to be slightly longer than a pro stop. The Federation language comes from the abandoned pro language of 1988, the year balks skyrocketed and the player's association rejected the change. I wouldn't worry about it; if you can discern a stop, that should be good enough.

NCAA also uses a complete stop, but goes on to say "a complete stop is an instantaneous stop and is interpreted as a complete change of direction of the hands." The physics of this is unarguable; in order to change direction 180 degrees, you must first stop. It does create a contradiction in the windup position where the pitcher must deliver "without interruption." If the pitcher pumps, he changes the direction of his hands and thereby stops or interrupts his motion. I don't suggest you try that logic on a coach!

Back to baseball. The effect of this rule is you will never call a balk in a college game because of the pitcher's failure to stop. In a Florida tournament last year, an umpire called such a balk on an Amherst College pitcher. The Amherst coach, Bill Thurston, who is also the NCAA rules editor, stormed out of the dugout, "That's not the rule." The chagrined umpire, recognizing his error, replied, "OK, the balk stands, but I won't call it again."

In the other codes, if you have to think about whether the pitcher stopped long enough, he did. If he's marginal, send the catcher or shortstop over to talk to him. The last thing you want to do is let him do it almost the entire game and then at a critical moment, call a balk. Please remember, the pitcher need not stop before picking-off, only before pitching.

Federation requires the stop to be with the glove below the chin, while pro and NCAA stipulate in front of the body. Does that mean in front of his nose is OK? Yes, in medical books, the head is part of the body. Back to the high school world. I once did a game out on the Eastern plains of Colorado where the home pitcher, Elton, only knew the set position and his favorite stopping point was his eyes. Elton made it through the first inning without a base runner, so there was no point in delaying the game for a tutorial. When he came out for the second inning, my partner and I had a chat with him. Elton did well that inning and for most of the third, but it was downhill from there. Old habits don't die easily; Elton soon went back to stopping at his eyes. On some pitches, he would realize his error and quickly jerk the ball below his chin for a second stop. By that time, Elton had given up at least a dozen runs and his team was hopelessly behind, so we let him finish the game his way.

Feints

The pitcher may feint to any occupied base except first. He may also feint or throw to an unoccupied base for the purpose of making a play i.e., a runner who has advanced prematurely. If he feints to first or throws or feints to an unoccupied base when there is no play, it is a balk (pro: 8.05b, NCAA: 9-3a, Fed: 6-2-4a).

Fielder off base

Sometimes a first baseman will miss a sign or just plain not be where's he's supposed to be or where the pitcher thinks he is. If a pitcher throws to a fielder who is not on the base, it is not a balk under Federation rules if the fielder is in "proximity" of the base and is not a balk under NCAA rules if the fielder is "relatively close" to the base. Both interpretations require umpire judgment. Under pro rules, the fielder must be at the base or it is a balk. A rule of thumb is to note whether the off-base fielder is surprised by the throw; if so, balk. If he can make it look like a play, let it go.

Step toward the base

On a pickoff to any base from the rubber, the pitcher must first step towards that base (pro: 8.01c, NCAA: 9-3c, Fed: 6-2-4b). The purpose of this rule is to slow down the pickoff move and give the runner a fighting chance. The pitcher must step in advance of the throw and his foot must come down more toward first than home. The line (defined in Federation and practical for the others) runs from the center of the rubber to a point halfway between home and first, where the three-foot lane begins. No one will ever draw it for you, so you must visualize it. If the pitcher's foot comes close to that line, but you're not sure, he stepped toward first. Please note none of the codes require the pitcher to step towards the plate when he pitches from the set position, so don't get confused over that one.

Left handers present a special challenge. Many believe a southpaw doesn't have to step toward first when picking. The basis for the misconception is that he is already facing first with his non-pivot foot pointing towards the base. In reality, the left hander must step directly towards first, as well as any other base, before throwing. The rules do not distinguish between righties and lefties. A guideline here is to insist the heel of the free foot gets at least as close to first base as the toe was when he started; that is a "step."

A local coach told me, "You may be right by the book, but no one ever calls it, so it's true." Once a season, I will run into a coach who believes the flat-footed throw to first is legal for his lefty. The last time I called that, the pitcher threw it over the first baseman's head and the runner made it to third. It was a high school game so I had to return the runner to second since the ball was dead on my balk call. The defensive coach thought I was nuts and would not accept my explanation. I was about to say "OK, you win; I'll put the runner on third," when he suddenly gave up the argument and trotted back to the dugout.

Direct step

If the pitcher fails to step directly to the base before throwing, he has balked. A good rule of thumb for righties is for the plate umpire to watch the free foot. If he can see the sole of the shoe, it is a balk. Why? For the sole to show, the pitcher rocked back as if to pitch and did not step directly to first. Please note, a jump turn is legal. A jump turn is where the pitcher alights with both feet simultaneously and gains ground toward first with his non-pivot foot. Purists will note the illegality of disengaging the rubber forward, but no one has ever written a totally consistent rulebook in any sport (pro: NAPBL 6.4f; NCAA: 9-3c-5; Fed: 6-1-3, 6.1.3i).

Shoulder turn

Those of us who work prep games spend a lot of time at the start of each season discussing the right-handed pitcher's shoulder and what he can and cannot do with regard to a runner on first. Although the restrictions on the pitcher begin when he intentionally engages the rubber in all three codes, any shoulder movement by a pitcher before he comes to a stop is not an infraction in NCAA and pro games. Under Federation rules, any shoulder movement, either before or after the stop, constitutes a feint if not followed immediately by a throw.

Abrupt movements must be penalized with the balk. Subtle movement due to breathing, fidgeting, etc., should be ignored. When you're in doubt, the pitcher's shoulder movement is not a feint. At any level, you do not want to penalize a pitcher for a simple glance toward the runner which fools no one. The purpose of the rule is obvious — to keep the pitcher from bouncing the runner back and forth merely by twitching his shoulder. Keep that in mind and you won't go wrong.

Back edge of rubber

Once the pitcher swings his entire free foot past the plane of the back edge of rubber, he is committed to pitch and cannot throw to first or throw or feint third (pro: 8.05a Comment, NCAA: 9-1b-3, Fed: 6-2-4f). Obviously, his foot must pass the back edge of the rubber for him to step toward second for a throw or feint to that base. That balk is extremely difficult to detect with only two umpires and it should be left to the base umpire. Again, use the sole of the shoe as a guide. If the base umpire can see the sole of the free foot as the pitcher kicks back, the pitcher has probably put his entire foot past the back edge of the rubber. Under NCAA rules, the above restriction also applies if any part of the stride leg (knee) breaks the plane (9-3L).

"31" move

Another popular pick is the "31" move, which requires the umpire's close attention. With runners on the corners, the pitcher bluffs a throw to third and then either throws or feints to first. I can count on one hand the number of times I have seen this work, but pitchers will persist. The first thing to look for is a step toward third; the pitcher must do that regardless of what follows. If he then only bluffs to first, his foot must be off the rubber. To this point, we haven't seen anything we haven't already discussed: stepping toward the base on a pick and disengaging the rubber before feinting to first.

What the 31 play allows, which is not ordinarily permissible, is disengaging the rubber by stepping forward. If the pitcher follows through and throws to first, the codes treat it differently. NCAA and pro: He must have disengaged the rubber. Federation: He may have kept his foot on the rubber, provided he stepped toward first. It is very difficult to keep the pivot foot on the rubber while doing all that and you'll probably never see it.

Knee flex

Now that you're an expert on twitching shoulders, let's talk about flexing knees. Only NCAA deals specifically with this topic, but it applies at all levels since we are dealing with an act which is part of the habitual pitching motion. The prohibition is on the pitcher prematurely flexing his leg before stepping and throwing to first. No one expects the pitcher to either pitch or pick with a stiff leg. If you judge the pitcher is using the same flex on both pitches and picks and by doing so, he is deceiving the runner, you should call a balk. If you have to intently analyze both moves to figure that out, you ought to leave it alone.

EITHER POSITION

Natural motion

With his foot on the rubber, the pitcher can balk if he makes any motion naturally associated with his delivery and fails to do so (Pro: 8.05a; NCAA: 9-3-a, g; Fed: 6-2-4a).

Facing batter

In pro and NCAA, the pitcher shall stand facing the batter (pro: 8.01a, NCAA: 9-1a). There is no penalty for an NCAA pitcher who violates; it is a balk in pro. In Federation and pro, the pitcher must face the batter when delivering. It is extremely difficult to look in one direction and throw in another. That rule was adopted in 1899 to prevent "freak" deliveries and has outlived it's usefulness. I've never seen a pitcher commit that balk and I don't think you will either (pro: 8.05f, Fed: 6-1-1).

Drops ball

The pitcher cannot drop the ball while on the rubber. If such a dropped ball passes a foul line, a ball is called; otherwise it is a balk. Those of us who believe in advantage/ disadvantage officiating cannot comprehend this rule. Nonetheless, it is a rule and is known by practically every kid who has ever played the game. Consequently, the infraction must be immediately called (pro: 8.05k, NCAA: 9-2b, Fed: 6-2-4a).

Disengages

The pitcher cannot disengage the rubber by stepping forward. I earlier discussed the exceptions to that: the jump turn and the "31" move. Additionally, he cannot disengage by first moving the free foot. Such movement is considered the start of either a pitch or pickoff attempt. The purpose of the rule is that when the pitcher's free foot moves forward, the runner is entitled to view it as the start of a pitch. If the free foot moves swiftly or as in the normal pitching motion, call the balk. If he is merely disengaging in a distracted manner or switching positions (see next section), I suggest you pass on it. Pro further requires the pitcher to drop his hands to his side after disengaging, but as long as he does that before re–engaging, there is no violation (pro: 8.01a Comment; NCAA: 9-1a-1c, 9-1b; Fed: 6-1-2, 6-1-3).

Switches positions

The next balk is one you could call at least once a week. The pitcher cannot move from the set position to the windup or vice versa without first properly disengaging the rubber as discussed above. Here's the play: Runner on second steals third; pitcher takes the set position. Coach yells from the dugout, "Use the windup." Where's the deception? What's the advantage? When you hear that, call "time" and avoid the issue (pro: 8.01a Comment, NCAA: 9-1a-5, Fed: 6-1-3).

Removes hand

Regardless of whether the pitcher has his hands together or apart, he cannot remove his hand from the ball other than to pitch or to pickoff (pro: 8.05j; NCAA: 9-1a-1a, b, c;, Fed: 6-2-4).

Defaced ball

Under pro rules, the pitcher may not under any circumstances, rub the ball on his glove, clothing or person. Penalty: ball. In NCAA and Federation, he may do so as long as the ball is not defaced. If the pitcher is caught with a defaced ball, but hasn't yet pitched it: Federation: a balk with runners and a ball without; NCAA and Pro: Warning, then ejection. If he pitches a defaced ball, the penalties are: Federation: a ball or balk; NCAA: warning only followed by ejection for repeated violations; pro: always a ball (Pro: 8.02a-4, NCAA: 9-2d, Fed: 6-2-1c).

Catcher balk

Surprisingly, the catcher can cause a balk by prematurely leaving the catcher's box. In Federation, he must have both feet in the box at the time of the pitch (1-1-3, 6-1-1). Under NCAA rules, he must stay until the ball leaves the pitcher's hand (5-4a, 9-3i). In pro, the catcher is only restricted during an intentional walk; he may leave his box when the ball leaves the pitcher's hand (4.03a, 8.05L). Under pro and NCAA rules, it is also a catcher balk if he interferes when a runner is stealing home or trying to score on a squeeze (NCAA: 8-30, Pro: 7.07).

Ambidextrous pitcher

In recent years, rules coverage has been added for ambidextrous pitchers. Only under NCAA rules can such a pitcher commit a balk by improperly switching hands. In the event I have you believing I've covered all the possibilities, try this. Sooner or later, you will come across a pitcher who will take a set position stance with no runners on and will windup or just not stop. What do you do? Hopefully, you now know enough to answer that on your own!

PROHIBITIONS

Now that you understand what a balk is, I'll wrap up this chapter by covering the general pitching prohibitions which are not balks. The items which are identical under the three codes are first and then, on to the rules differences.

Glove color

The pitcher's glove must meet the size specifications for a fielder's glove and cannot be white, gray or multicolored. There are manufactured gloves with checkered black and tan webbing. Those are technically illegal for pitchers, but I've never gotten a complaint. If an illegal glove is used, the offender should be directed to replace it and can be ejected if he refuses to comply.

Foreign substance

The pitcher is prohibited from applying a foreign substance to the ball to include spitting on the ball or glove. Earlier I discussed the penalty if the ball is defaced. If the foreign substance does not deface the ball, a warning is given with ejection for a subsequent offense.

Distracting items

Under Federation and NCAA rules, the pitcher may not wear distracting items on his arms, wrists or hands. There is no rules provision in pro, but the umpire should use his 9.01c authority to have any distracting item removed. NCAA prohibits the pitcher from wearing a batting or golf glove under his fielder's glove. Federation allows one as long as it is the same color or darker than the fielder's glove.

Jewelry is not a problem in Federation games because jewelry on all players is prohibited. In NCAA and pro games, the umpire must determine whether the item is distracting. There are various other items which the batter may claim are distracting such as wrist bands, etc. The interpretations generally state that if a batter complains about a distracting item, frivolous requests excluded, the umpire should have it removed.

Tape and bandages

Federation rules prohibit a pitcher from having tape or bandages on his pitching fingers or palm. NCAA rules prohibit tape on the fingers only. An NCAA pitcher also may not have different colored tape on either his uniform or glove. There are no restrictions under pro rules. The penalty is a warning with ejection for a subsequent offense.

Undershirt sleeves

The pitcher's undershirt sleeves must be about the same length. In a Federation game, they cannot be white or gray. In an NCAA game, they cannot be white. Under pro rules, there are no color restrictions, but almost everyone believes they cannot be white. You should decide if they are "distracting" and have them removed if necessary.

Throwing close to batter

The pitcher may not intentionally pitch at the batter. The penalty is a warning followed by ejection for subsequent offenses. NCAA rules have a specific procedure for the umpire to take following a suspected bean ball. The umpire warns the pitcher and both coaches that any pitcher for either team who commits the next offense will be ejected, along with the head coach (9-2f Pen). In unusual circumstances the umpire may: (1) warn both teams before the game; or (2) eject the pitcher without warning; or (3) eject the coach without warning if he feels that is appropriate.

A pitcher ejected for throwing at a batter is considered a "suspended" player, subject to the penalties under the provisions of the fight rule (9-2f Pen 3). The penalty: First offense: ejection and suspension from the team's next four games. Second offense by the same pitcher in the same season: ejection and suspension from the team's next eight games. Third offense by the same pitcher in the same season: ejection and suspension for the remainder of the season, including postseason play (5-15d).

QUIZ

The following 10 questions will test your knowledge of pitching regulations. In each of the following you are given a situation and at least two possible answers. You are to decide which answer or answers are correct for Federation, NCAA and pro rules, which might vary. Note: R1 is a runner on first, etc.

1. Bottom of ninth with the visiting team leading, 2-1. Runner on third. The pitcher balks and immediately delivers to B1. B1 hits a homerun over the fence. The umpire calls the balk and:

    a. The ball is dead, R3 scores, no pitch.

    b. The ball is dead, R3 scores, a ball is awarded B1.

    c. The ball remains live, game over, home team wins, 3-2.

2. With runners on the corners, the pitcher balks but delivers immediately. The pitch hits B1.

    a. B1 remains at bat.

    b. B1 is awarded first.

    c. R1 remains at first.

    d. R1 is awarded second.

    e. R3 remains at third.

    f. R3 scores.

3. With the bases loaded and a 3-2 count on the batter, the pitcher balks but delivers immediately. The pitch is called ball four.

    a. B1 remains at bat.

    b. Each runner is awarded on base on the balk.

    c. The play stands.

4. With a runner at third, the pitcher assumes a windup stance. Before making any other movement, with his pivot foot on the rubber, he steps towards third and throws there.

    a. Legal.

    b. Legal, but a feint would have been illegal.

    c. Illegal, call a balk.

    d. Illegal, call a ball.

5. With a runner on first, the pitcher takes a set position stance. The first baseman holds the runner on by standing with both feet completely in foul territory.

a. Legal.

b. The fielder must have at least one foot in fair territory.

c. The fielder must have both feet in fair territory.

d. It is a balk if a pitch is made.

6. With runners on the corners, the pitcher takes a set position stance. The pitcher begins his stretch, but he drops the ball.

a. The ball is immediately dead when it is dropped.

b. If the ball stops before it crosses a foul line, it is a balk.

c. If the ball rolls across a foul line, it is a ball.

7. With two out, no runners on base and a 3-2 count on the batter, the pitcher delivers from the set position and B1 swings and misses.

a. Legal, strike out stands.

b. Balk.

c. Illegal pitch, ball four.

8. With a runner on first, the pitcher takes a set position stance. Before his delivery, he stands motionless and changes the direction (180 degrees) of his hands, but does not come to a discernible stop. B1 swings and misses.

a. Legal.

b. Balk.

c. A ball is awarded.

9. With F1 in a set position, F2 calls a pitch out. R1 breaks for second and F2 steps out of the catcher's box after F1 breaks his hands from the stop, but before he releases the ball.

a. Legal.

b. Balk.

c. A ball is awarded.

10. With no runners, F1 takes his sign while standing behind the rubber. He then steps forward, begins his windup and delivers.

a. Legal.

b. Balk.

c. A ball is awarded.

d. A warning is given.

ANSWERS

1 — **pro** - **c** (8.05 Penalty), **NCAA** - **c** (9-3 Pen 1), **Fed** - **a** (5-1-1k, 6-1 Penalty)

2 — **All** - **a, d, f** (pro 8.05 Pen, NCAA 9-3 Penalty, Fed 5-1-1k, 6-1 Penalty)

3 — **pro** - **c** (8.05 Penalty), **NCAA** - **c** (9-3 Penalty), **Fed** - **a, b** (5-1-1k,6-1 Penalty)

4 — **pro** - **a** (8.01a), **NCAA** - **a** (9-1a), **Fed** - **c** (6-1-2)

5 — **pro** - **a** (4.03), **NCAA** - **b** (5-4), **Fed** - **b, d** (1-1-3)

6 — **All** - **b, c** (pro 8.05k, NCAA 9-2b, Fed 6-2-4a)

7 — **All** - **a** (pro 8.01, NCAA 9-1, Fed 6-1-1)

8 — **pro** - **b** (8.01b, 8.05e Penalty), **NCAA** - **a** (9-1b-2), **Fed** - **b** (6-1-3 Penalty)

9 — **pro** - **a** (4.03a, 8.05L), **NCAA** - **b** (5-4a, 9-3i), **Fed** - **a** (1-1-3,6-1-1)

10 — **pro** - **d** (8.01), **NCAA** - **c** (7-5d), **Fed** - **c** (6-1-1 Penalty)

4

Admitting Mistakes

By George Demetriou

Dwayne Finley, Sylmar, Calif.

One of the dilemmas which all officials face is whether to admit to a mistake. That is one of the few facets of officiating which is markedly different between the professional and amateur worlds. Major League umpires are ingrained to never acknowledge an error. AL umpire Jim Evans told me "they'll eat you alive" if you admit to a mistake.

In the amateur climate, it's a different story. In a March 1996 *Referee* feature titled "Getting Along," Jim Gilbert, a four-sport official from Utah, advised honesty is the only policy. I can certainly relate to that. Having graduated from West Point where there is zero tolerance for "lying, cheating and stealing" and having lived under that mantra for a 23-year military career, I can personally attest to the merits of that way of life.

Every rule has exceptions. In the West Point Honor Code, the exception is tabbed "social honor." A very basic example is telling a woman her dress looks lovely when it looks like she slept in it. Deception is an essential element of warfare. These two items put together form the basis for the cliché "All is fair in love and war." How then can these concepts be applied to umpiring?

Basketball uses the term: "correctable error." The baseball equivalent is a rules application error. An incorrect base award, is perhaps the most frequent occurrence. In such a situation, if your partner pulls you aside or a coach protests, don't hesitate to review what you've done and, if you made an error, admit it and fix it. When the correct answer is the end result, the fact a mistake was initially made normally will quickly be forgotten.

There are situations when it is permissible to change a call. The plate umpire appealing to a base umpire on a checked swing can result in the change of a judgment call from ball to strike. That is such an accepted procedure almost no one thinks of it as changing a call or the commission of an error. Other situations where changing a judgment call is permissible include a dropped ball after a tag

There are situations when it is permissible to change a call.

and when opposite calls are made by two umpires. In those situations, you should by all means acknowledge and correct the error.

Swipe tags and pulled foots are not normally situations where a call can be reversed. The proper procedure is to get help before making the call. At some levels though, it is acceptable to change such a call; proceed with care. The risk is opening the door to an endless stream of requests to "get help." You are also susceptible to the coach on the short end of the reversal saying, "Once you call it, you're supposed to live with it."

Other judgment calls — safe or out, fair or foul — cannot be reversed. In such situations, you run the risk of inflaming the situation by confessing to having erroneously altered the course of history. I'll stop short of an absolute edict, because it does depend on the exact game situation and the personalities of the coaches, but extreme caution is advised. Here's a situation, where I "confessed" in the interest of moving the game along and only aggravated the situation.

In a late-season 1995 game between league rivals with playoff elimination at stake, I was behind the plate. In the fourth inning, the home coach, down by six, claimed the opposing pitcher had balked. I was very polite, "Coach, what did you see him do?" After listening to a lengthy and largely incoherent diatribe, I replied, "I didn't see that, but I'll check." My partner likewise, did not observe the alleged felony. "Coach, neither one of us saw that and we can't call what we didn't see." It was now clear all the coach wanted to do was exact a pound of flesh. "He's not the issue, you're supposed to be watching for that, now call it." After several more exchanges which repeated the previous statements, I finally stated, "OK, Coach, I blew it. Now let's play ball." I had played into his hands. "You *blew* it! I'm out here trying to win a game and you're blowing calls?" He ranted and raved for awhile and finally calmed down.

There are situations in the amateur world where it makes sense to acknowledge an error or at least allude to the possibility you may have missed the call. If you don't, you run the risk of coming across as inflexible, unyielding and arrogant. There are limits and I'm not saying you should eagerly confess every error.

There are situations in the amateur world where it makes sense to acknowledge an error.

We all miss pitches and when the catcher asks, "What was wrong with that?" it's OK to reply, "Nothing." On fair/foul or safe/out controversies, you might try, "That's the way I saw it, but if it happens again, I might rule the other way." Of course, you can't do either of these more than once or twice a game.

In Limon, Colo., as in many fields around the country, the lights are on telephone poles outside the field. Once every 10 years, a fair ball will hit the light pole and rebound back onto the field. That happened in a 1996 game with no one out and runners on first and second. The base umpire, unsure of whether the ball hit the fence or pole, kept the ball in play. R2 trotted home thinking homerun and was nabbed at the plate. The protests was vicious and the umpires consulted. They upheld the ruling by saying the ball hit off the fence. The batter and R1 subsequently scored. When the center fielder came in, the plate umpire asked for the truth and got it — they got the play wrong. Focusing on the two runs scored and forgetting about the play at the plate, the umpire acknowledged the error to the offended coach. That only served to reopen the protests and resulted in a very ugly game. The offended team lost, 6-4, so the impact of the error can never be discerned.

Here's a situation where a tight-lipped umpire avoided aggravating the situation. In a 1997 regional final (final eight), Skyline High School (Longmont, Colo.) was at bat in the top of the second with a runner on first and one out. The sacrifice bunt was excellent and F1 was very slow in getting off the mound. The base umpire's initial thought was there was no play. Nonetheless, he started to position himself for a throw to first. Instead, the

Durango High School pitcher fired a bullet to second. Again, the base umpire's predisposition was "safe by a mile." The throw was to the shortstop side of the bag and the fielder had to stretch for it, but he kept his foot on the bag. R1 must have had the same anticipation as the umpire for he had slowed down and gone into the base standing up. The throw beat the runner by at least half a step, but inexplicably the base umpire hollered, "safe."

As soon as his tongue stopped moving, he knew he had blown it. The crowd jeered. The Durango coach, to his credit, kept his cool, calmly walking out, "What is going on here?" "Coach, it was a close play and I called him safe." "No, that's not good enough. I think you thought he pulled his foot." (An effort to make the case for an appeal.) "No, I saw he kept his foot on the base. It was just close and I called him safe." As the coach left he got the last word in: "It wasn't really that close." The next batter homered, so the gaffe cost Durango a run.

The base umpire got off easy. He never lied nor did he admit the error. A confession would have served no purpose; that call simply could be changed. Perhaps considering the rare gentlemanly approach of the Durango coach and his apparent acceptance of the finality of the call, the base umpire could have admitted the mistake and promised to do better, but, as in the other examples, that could also have set off the entire Durango squad. An umpire's nightmare is to eject a coach who has been screwed by an error.

An umpire's nightmare is to eject a coach who has been screwed by an error.

A related issue is whether an official should ever apologize for a mistake. Although not a frequent occurrence, coaches have been known to demand apologizes. On at least one occasion, a coach has demanded the erring official apologize to the entire team.

Several years ago, a normally mild mannered umpire called the third out on a fly ball. The center fielder came trotting in with the ball and flipped it to the umpire with excessive force, hitting the arbiter in the chin. That act drew a targeted profanity from the umpire to the player. The player told his coach who immediately came out and demanded an apology to the entire team in the dugout. The umpire refused, but agreed to apologize to the offended player when he came back out.

No matter what the situation, when responding to such requests, the official must be careful to not trivialize the matter. A possible response is "Coach, I've acknowledged the error and that's as far as I'm going to go."

5

Rise
Above It All

By Bill Topp

BOB MESSINA

Plate umpire,
Shawn Talbott,
Hermosa Beach, Calif.

"Sometimes, the most wonderful thing about this game is that it stunts your growth" — then Oakland A's pitcher Dennis Eckersley, in Mike Lupica's *The Sporting News* column, August 28, 1995

Getting the "big" game and the "big" game goes awry

It's three months before the season and you finally get your assignments for the upcoming year. You've been waiting anxiously to see the teams you'll be working for. In the back of your mind, you're praying you don't have to see Coach Loudmouth and begging for a chance to work "the big one."

You tear open the envelope and peer over the games. There it is! You've landed the big one! You've got two perennial powers pitted against each other; it's the game everyone who is anyone in the area wants. You've worked hard for it. Hey, this means you've arrived! You're like a kid in a candy store as you race to the phone to call your partner.

Six months have passed and "the big game" is finally here. You're juiced up and fighting to keep emotions in check. The standing room only crowd is frenzied before the game. This shapes up to be a great game!

Guess again. The home team leaps out to an insurmountable lead and the game is a rout. You can actually feel the game deflate as the crowd, the players and the coaches sense the game is over within the first few minutes. You are disappointed and your concentration wanes while the game drones through the final period. Suddenly, harsh words are exchanged among players as frustration sets in and you react too late. A fight erupts, players are ejected and coaches are blaming you for the game being out of control. You can't help but think how all your umpiring "buddies" with "I told you so" attitudes are thinking you couldn't handle the game. The "big game" has gone south and you went with it.

The solution

Develop an "every game is a big one" attitude. That is not easy to do, especially for the competitive umpires who measure success by the number of games or the records of the teams playing. Sure you enjoy the challenge of officiating, but, the games truly are for the participants, especially the kids playing. You are only a small — albeit important — part of the game. The quicker you realize that, the better attitude you'll have toward all your games.

Remember this: most anyone can work the well-played games. It's the well-handled, poorly played games that separate great officials from average ones. When the game's score or sloppiness gets out of hand, great officials turn it up a notch and finish strong.

Heavy rules preparation followed by a rules error

You are a rulebook guru. Whenever a local umpire has a rules question, your phone rings. You probably should install a 900 phone number so at least you can make some money doing it, but you love talking rules. You've got five copies of the rulebook and study at least 15 minutes every day. In fact, you've got a rulebook sitting on the back of the toilet so you can study during those "down" times!

In the heat of a well-played game, a somewhat strange play happens, though you've seen the play before. You make the call and the coach goes crazy. "He doesn't know the rule," you think as you administer penalties swiftly. Your partner hesitantly approaches you to verbally replay the play and ends his last sentence with, "Are you sure?"

"Of course I'm sure," you fire back. Your body language exudes confidence while inside you're starting to question yourself. The ruling has major impact on the outcome of the game.

After the game, you race to the rulebook to prove to your partner that you're the rulesmaster. There it is, in black and white. You were *wrong*! A sudden sickness envelopes you. You slump down in your chair, knowing that you may have cost a team the game and severely damaged your reputation as the all-knowing guru. "I've read that millions of times before. How could I have made that mistake?" you think to yourself. Your partner tries to cheer you up, to no avail.

The solution
Forget about it for now and remember it for next time it happens. Unless you've got a 32-megabytes-of-computer-ram-brain, you are not likely to remember every possible scenario that could happen in a game.

Don't go flushing your rulebook down the toilet! The best thing to take into your next game is to talk things out with your partner (or yourself) if either of you is even the slightest bit unsure. Penalty administration is not a race and sometimes slowing things down mentally can help you avoid errors. Remember, no one is perfect. It's the strive for perfection that makes us better.

Young stud rising faster

You, as they say, are "the man." You're the guy that walks into Wednesday night association meetings and all in attendance begin whispering to each other, "There *he* is." You're the best in the area and, even though you don't seek the fanfare, you enjoy it somewhat. You've worked hard at it for the last 20 years and are simply reaping some side benefits. The scuttlebutt is you're going to state again and you're a lock to move up to higher levels of games in the next few years.

In the group is a young, athletic, All-American looking guy who just a few years ago finished a stellar playing career at State University and began officiating to stay in the game. You hear he's a natural, but you're not worried because he's so young and just getting started.

The next year, the young stud attends a few camps and impresses some of the higher-ups. He lands a big prep game as a fill-in when an official gets hurt. "They must not have asked me because I've had those teams before," you think to yourself, justifying the slight. The young stud has a great game, makes some tough calls down the stretch and is instantly revered by the umpiring power players.

A few college coaches were in the stands for that game scouting some players. They noticed the young stud from his playing days and thought it was great to see someone that played so well at such a high level get into umpiring. They were so impressed with his composure and skill that the coaches called the college conference office the next day to recommend him. A few positive letters from camp directors later and the young stud has flown right by you as if you were standing still on his way to college games.

His meteoric rise crushes you're ego. You're no longer the talk of the town and the games you're working don't seem quite as exciting.

The solution

Instead of competing with other umpires, help them achieve their own levels of success. Develop a commitment to *the game* you umpire. When you think about improving the game as a whole, you'll realize the more good umpires there are in your area, the better the game will be. Take pride in the fact that you helped someone become a better umpire — maybe even better than yourself. If you're only in umpiring for you, you'll likely have a miserable existence in umpiring. Your over-competitive and jealous nature will catch up to you. Keep working hard at your game too and — to borrow and old cliché — let the chips fall where they may. You and the game will be better for it.

SIX THINGS TO THINK ABOUT

1. Think before the game

Time and time again, you've heard how important a pregame conference with your partner is. Why? The time before the game is the time to sort out problems that could occur during the game. By having a quality pregame discussion about rules, coverage, mechanics, philosophy, context, etc., you're ready when something happens.

First, you must really believe that a pregame conference is a good thing. If you're just going through the motions and not thinking about what's being discussed, you're likely to go through the motions during the game as well.

Don't fool yourself into thinking your pregame can solve all the problems you may encounter during your game. Your pregame should hit the high points and get you are your partner thinking alike.

2. Think before the play

The best officials always seem to be in the right place at the right time. Wonder how? They think about a play just before it happens.

Your brain must process a ton of information in an instant to make a call. Give your brain a little help by think about what may occur ahead of time. Talk to yourself about each play and run through possible scenarios.

Here's an example. "Tie score, a runner on third, late in the game. What could happen? The runner at third has good speed and the hitter is the best bunter on the team. Possible suicide squeeze. If it happens, here's what I'm going to do …."

Think about the rules that could be relevant to a particular play. Quickly whisk through the pertinent rules so that when the play happens, your brain has a jump start on sorting it out correctly.

3. Think like a coach

When effectively thinking before the play, you must think like a coach. Ask yourself, "What are the coach's options in this situation?" You want to think like the coach *involved in the play* , not necessarily as if *you* were the coach. Why? If it's you doing the coaching, your going to say, "Here's what I'd do ...." That's irrelevant! You should ask, "What is *he* going to do?" What the coach does may be in stark contrast to what you'd do if you were the coach, but if you consistently second-guess the coach's moves, you ought to just become one. Second-guessing coaches hurts your umpiring. You're not passing judgment on a coach's decisions, you're simply preparing yourself for different scenarios based on the coach's decisions.

4. Think like a player

Some umpires are very good because they were hellions as players. Why? As a player, they worked hard at getting away with things when umpires weren't watching. Now as umpires, they understand that some players today will try to get away with the same things, only the hellion-turned-ump is ready for it.

You must think like a player as a villain, as a strategist and as a competitor. That way, you won't be surprised when something happens. The more scenarios you play in your mind, the more you'll be ready when they occur.

5. Think before you speak

That sounds like something you were told in kindergarten, but it reigns true. Speak to people like you'd expect to be spoken to. If you scream at a coach or player, what gives you the right to get upset when coaches or players scream at you?

Before you even open your mouth, think about whether what is being said to you needs a response. You don't have to respond to everything that's said to you. Let most of it go and react to certain situations you think need attention.

Think about the tone of your own language and the manner in which you speak. Yelling, "Coach, shut your mouth!" with hands on your hips leaning forward will almost always earn a negative reaction (right now or later on). Saying, "Coach, I hear you and understand what you're saying" with hands behind your back in a less-combative posture may turn the conversation in a positive direction.

6. Think before you penalize

Think ahead to the possible outcomes of penalizing players and coaches. During the games, the thought process is very fast when making judgments but mentally gathering information is still vital. Did the contact impact the play? Was the contact severe? Is a gentle word better than a penalty?

Generally, you've got a little bit more time to think before doling out unsportsmanlike fouls or ejections. Think ahead to the possible scenarios. You've got to get something positive back when doling out a penalty. Ask yourself, "If I penalize that player for his behavior, will it help the game?" Or, "If I don't penalize that player, will the situation escalate into something worse?"

No umpires are allowed to carry crystal balls with them when they work games; thinking ahead is the next best thing. If you can master the art of talking to yourself while officiating, you'll be better prepared.

How much should you know about teams?

Part of good pregame preparation is gaining knowledge about participants. That theory summates that an official who is prepared has a good chance of successfully dealing with situations.

But how far does that statement go? Should officials know everything about a particular team or game? How does that impact the way you deal with situations during the game?

There is a fine line between preparation and pre-programming. On the surface it would seem the more information you have, the better prepared you will be. That is true. You want information so you can better understand why things are happening and properly deal with them.

The dangerous flip-side is letting the information you've gathered negatively influence the way you handle a situation. Here are a couple of examples to illustrate the point. The first is how information can help; the second, how it can hurt.

Prepared

You've been assigned to umpire a baseball game between cross-town rivals. Because you're familiar with the history of the rivalry, you know there's been trouble between the two in the past. The teams and coaches (heck, even the towns) don't like each other. Due to that history, you correctly ascertain there's likely to be a lot of emotion in the game, probably more than your typical game.

You've heard through the umpiring grapevine that last year when the teams played, a bench-clearing brawl erupted. The threats of "payback" were often heard.

As an umpire, you want that type of information. It is critical to understanding the context of the game. You're less likely to get surprised by unseemly events. Certainly, you want to be prepared for "bad blood" between teams in every game you work, but having detailed, history-laden information helps you and your crew properly focus on the potential problems before they happen.

In a situation like that, you may need to deal with things differently than you would in a "normal" situation. For example, what might be an innocuous comment by a player to another player in a normal setting might not get a strong reaction from that player. The umpires would likely use preventive officiating and talk to the player who did the talking to make sure it doesn't develop into a problem. That same comment in an emotion-filled game might draw a more volatile reaction by the player. Because the umpire has the proper context, the umpire should deal with the problem in a more stern manner, using stronger language with the player or even penalizing without warning if necessary to control the situation.

It could be argued that is inconsistent from one game to the other. That in fact is true. Good umpires understand game context and adjust accordingly. No games are exactly the same; if they were, there'd be little reason to play them. No situation for officials is exactly the same either. Having good information prior to a game gives you the proper context to handle things appropriately *for that game.*

Pre-programming

Here's a situation where information negatively pre-programs an umpire. Through the umpire grapevine, you hear stories from other umps about how baseball coach John Doe at Anywhere High School is a real jerk. According to the umpires, Coach Doe is mean, constantly berating umpires and tries to intimidate. "I dumped (ejected) the coach last year," you hear from one ump. "I should've this year. If I ever see him again, I'm going to get it done this time," says another.

You've been assigned to umpire at Anywhere High School a week after you've heard those comments. You've never had a game with that coach before.

In the first inning, Coach Doe shouts, "Where was that pitch?" on a close call. Without hesitation, you rip off your mask, stride forcefully toward Coach Doe and say, "You're not going to intimidate me tonight! Don't even think of trying it!"

Clearly, because of the negative information gathered before the game, the umpire became pre-programmed. The comment from the coach likely didn't even deserve a response and the umpire over-reacted because of the pre-programming.

Knowing that "word on the street" says Coach Doe is a jerk is not the problem; knowing that gives you context and understanding. The problem is letting that information influence you in a negative way.

The amount of knowledge you gain about a particular team, player, coach or game is a fine line. Gain enough to help you understand why things are happening in the game. Be mature and responsible enough to sort through the information and treat each game as a new one. Use the information as another tool to help you do your job effectively.

Unity in adversity

Be positive. Sounds so simple, yet it can be so difficult to do. Because of the rat race that sometimes accompanies climbing the officiating ladder and getting more and better assignments, we forget that as officials, we really are all in it together.

If you're truly an official, not someone who simply officiates, you feel for the officials you watch on TV and at least in some small way understand the pressures they face. You root for them, maybe not outwardly, but you hope that all goes well for them, just like you hope your youth game tomorrow goes equally smooth. No matter the level or the sport, in its simplest form, it's all the same.

That's why it's critical we work together. The old cliché that says you're only as strong as your weakest link applies to officiating. You may be one of the better officials in your area, but if the rest around you are weak, the game in your area suffers. The game is what's important. Do your best to help that "weak link" become strong. The give-back relationship that you develop with other officials will last for generations.

The following item was written by Randy Parker, a baseball umpire from Auburn, Calif. Though written about a baseball game, the lessons Parker learned that day from a cherished veteran apply to all sports at all levels.

Standing together

If I live to be 1000, I will always remember my first Big League game at James Field. My partner was Bob Harris. We worked a doubleheader on a typically hot summer Sunday in Auburn, Calif.

I was terrible and I knew it! I made a lot of rookie mistakes throughout both games. My timing was so quick on one pitch that I rang up a strike right before the batter hit it for a double! On another close pitch, I yelled out "ball" very loudly as I raised my right hand signaling strike! Squirming out of that situation was quite amusing and Harris an I still get a good laugh reminiscing. My game on the bases was not much better, either. I'm sure that I only kicked about five or six calls. Fortunately, I only had about seven or eight close ones. I think you get the picture.

Afterwards, I was so sure that Bob was going to criticize me for my many mistakes that I tried to sneak out of the park very quickly and quietly after the game. After all, I already knew how terrible I was. I certainly did not need him to rub it in!

He was quick. He caught up with me and he knew that I knew that we were supposed to do a postgame critique, so, I was stuck. I was about to raked over the coals. After all, he was a 20-plus year Little League baseball umpire. As far as I knew, he was probably the greatest Big League umpire in all of California. After all, his game did go as smooth as silk, especially in comparison. I was in way over my head anyway. I was certain that he was about to tell me that some umpires should probably stay in the Senior League or maybe even lower (much lower) for, well, perhaps their entire careers.

I braced for the worst. I'll never forget his first words. *He asked me*, "What do you think *I* could do to improve?" After I picked myself up off the ground, I asked him to repeat his question and he said it again. "What do you think *I* could do to improve?" I was speechless! How could he be asking me a question like that? What was I supposed to say? I was so focused on my own insecurities and inabilities that ...

He went on to compliment me on things that I did well. He taught me how to sandwich criticism. I'm sure he must have criticized something I had done, but to this day, the only think I can remember about that postgame critique is how I felt. I felt proud that he acknowledged the few things I did right. I felt happy that Bob believed that I was worth helping. Most importantly, though, I felt honored that someone whom I held in such high regard would ask *me* to critique *him*. Bob Harris taught me how to be a partner that afternoon.

He could have ripped me up one side and down the other. He could have confirmed my suspicions that I needed many, many more years in the lower levels. Instead, Bob chose to be humble. He chose to be a good-finder. He chose to lift me up. He chose to remember that we had just finished participating in a game. Finally, he carefully, yet surreptitiously, chose to give me my first "brotherhood of officials" lesson.

I dream of the day when all involved in sports officiating will teach, preach and most importantly, be a shining example of the "brotherhood of officials." Unfortunately, the game is not designed to provide official recognition for a job well done. Therefore, it becomes our duty to stand together, on and off the field, regardless of our personal views. Umpires must enjoy "unity in adversity."

Believe in officiating

We all know officiating is a tough business. If it was easy, everyone would do it.

There are many pitfalls that mentally weigh on us: lack of

quality assignments, unprofessional partners, time away from home and family, association politics, coaches scratch lists… the list goes on and on. Each one is a reason to quit officiating. In fact, many that do quit cite those things and others as major factors.

The hard truth is, those things equate to ready-made excuses for failure. The umpiring business is no different than life itself: there are good days and bad days. Those that quit umpiring without really getting into it have probably moved on to something else in their lives. Odds are, they'll quit that too.

We've got so many people beating us up mentally in umpiring that it can be difficult to see the job through. Have you ever asked yourself in anger after an especially tough game, "Who needs umpiring?" When you stop and think about all that umpiring gives to you, the answer is, "You do."

Umpiring gives you a chance to shape the lives of young people. It gives you a chance to remain active in a sport you love. It gives you a chance to ensure ethics, sportsmanship and fair play remain important factors in your life and the lives of others. It gives you a chance to be a positive role model. It teaches you responsibility, work ethic and professionalism. If you're really into umpiring, umpiring gets into you. Fight through the critics and cynics that eat at us daily in our officiating worlds. You are performing an admirable service for others by giving of yourself.

It's OK to have bad days and poor thoughts about officiating. That's human nature. Just turn those negatives into positives. When you're down, read this list; you'll stay on the right track as a quality person and, in turn, a model official.

Be receptive

Sometimes are biggest problems come from other people. We don't like our ego bruised. Even people with extremely strong personalities hurt once in a while.

The key to being receptive is considering the source. "You're terrible!" coming from an overbearing, loud-mouthed Little League mother shouldn't get much attention in your mind because the source is not credible. Conversely, you become a better official, and a better person, if you are receptive to thoughts and ideas coming from people whom you respect. Open your mind every so often to listen to new concepts and consider other people's opinions. The survivors are those who adapt to change.

Be honest

Unreal expectations places extra burden in an already intense job. You must be honest with yourself about your abilities. Thinking that you're going to be a major league umpire one day is not a bad thought... unless you realistically don't have the ability or you've set an unrealistic time frame. The sooner you're honest with yourself about what exactly it is you want out of officiating, the more relaxed you'll become. You'll reach an inner peace that means mental comfort each time you take the field.

Become a leader

Too often, officiating becomes an "every man for himself" endeavor, with officials backstabbing and undercutting each other for assignments and promotions. Don't fall into the trap.

If you adopt the philosophy that you're going to help *others* reach their goals, you will reach yours. By become a leader, you can encourage people to work hard and do the right things to make themselves successful. In turn, you're raising expectations for them and for yourself. Learn to love helping people. Those you help are better, you're better and the game is better for it.

Be passionate

You've got to love what you're doing, or you really shouldn't be doing it. Look forward to your next assignment to see if you can meet its challenges and exceed your expectations. Let officiating get inside you to the point that it becomes a lifestyle. If you're passionate about integrity, honesty and professionalism, you've improved your quality of life. Is that worth getting passionate about? Absolutely!

Be courageous

It takes tons of courage to rise above it all and do the right thing. Doing what is right— versus what's popular or safe— takes strong will and conviction. You've got to believe in your heart that what you're doing is the right thing. When you do make a mistake (and you *will* make mistakes!), it takes great strength and courage to bounce back and learn from it. Give it your best at all times, never stop learning and stand tall through adversity— all life lessons shared in officiating.

Be persistent

Set attainable goals and work to reach them. A goal is simply a dream with a deadline. Adopt the Nike slogan, "Just Do It," into your everyday life. If you treat officiating like a business that you enjoy, you will be persistent in seeing the job through. Wake up everyday thinking, "How am I going to improve officiating today?" Maybe it's study the rulebook, watch a young official, work on a new mechanic, recruit a person to try officiating, thank someone who has helped you. With the mindset that you are going to improve umpiring everyday, you're going to do the little things necessary to improve our entire avocation and help yourself in the process.

Be self-disciplined

Along with being persistent, you've got to be self-disciplined. No one can or should hold your hand everyday in officiating. You can't rely on others to do the work for you. The only real way to help others and help yourself is to establish goals, set deadlines and be productive. Again, think of umpiring as a business and yourself as a business owner. By developing a business owner mentality, you will be self-disciplined because you have the will to succeed. Don't put things off until tomorrow; do it today and move onto other positive things tomorrow.

Have unshakable faith

The world is full of energy drag. The nightly news... the daily paper... the constant griping at work...pressure builds constantly and negative energy saps your strength. Add to that all of the umpiring woes and it's no wonder you don't want to do anything!

If you have unshakable faith that what you're doing improves others and yourself, there really are no "umpiring woes." Yes, there are challenges, but challenges met are akin to success. Believe that umpiring is a positive force in your life because it is. Most importantly, believe in yourself. You deserve it because you're a *real* official.

Baseball Umpires' Guidebook - Volume I, Proper Positioning

The most comprehensive book on umpire positioning available anywhere. Complete with positioning diagrams, end-of-chapter quizzes, and caseplays covering proper positioning for every situation! Information is presented in a clear, easy-to-read workbook format. You'll learn where to be, when and (most important) *why!*

Includes: Where to start each play • Where to go when the ball is hit • What to watch for and why • The latest two-umpire crew innovations • Helpful tips to make difficult coverage easier • Complete explanations why each position recommended is better than its alternatives • A solid review of each umpire's positioning responsibilities and priorities • More than 60 case situations with complete breakdowns for both umpires • Case studies, reviews and quiz materials to help you measure comprehension. (paperback, 166 pages)
BBUGVI, $19.95, NASO-Member Price: $15.95

Baseball Umpires' Guidebook - Volume II, Communications and Mechanics

Part two of the ideal training system for umpires at any level. Presents step-by-step information about **where** you are supposed to go during a play, **what** you have to do to insure you effectively cover the action working in a crew of two, and **why** many of the seemingly "little" things are so important.

Perfect preparation for any level! Includes: Communication and mechanics keys with the latest two-umpire crew innovations • Helpful tips to make difficult situations easier • Complete explanations of why recommended coverage is better than the alternatives • A solid review of each umpire's communication and mechanics responsibilities • More than 60 case situations with complete breakdowns for both umpires, including run-downs. (paperback, 169 pages)
BBUGV2, $19.95, NASO-Member Price: $15.95

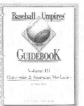

Baseball Umpires' Guidebook - Volume III, Three-man & Four-man Mechanics

Whether you work a full schedule of college three-umpire games or you're preparing for an end-of-the-season tournament that will use four-umpire crews, this is the reference book that provides the information you'll need to "get ready."

Includes: A basic discussion of the different responsibilities assigned to each umpire on three- and four-umpire crews • A review of basic on-field rotations — where to go, when, why, and what to look for • A conversational approach to trouble areas — plays that do happen, and do present coverage problems for three- and four-umpire crews • Clean, concise three- and four-umpire pregame outlines to help lead the discussion and coordinate the crew's efforts • Case studies. The now-familiar presentation of plays and coverages that have established this series of books as the quality standard in baseball mechanics. You'll find a step-by-step explanation of what each umpire does — complete with full-field diagrams — for dozens of play scenarios. (paperback, 211 pages) **BBUGV3, $19.95, NASO-Member Price: $15.95**

**Order the complete Baseball Umpires' Guidebook series —
Volumes I, II and III— together in a three-ring binder for $59.95!
NASO members pay just $47.95!**
All information is presented in a clear, easy-to-read workbook format
with detailed graphics, explanations, reviews and quizzes. Each vol-
ume is printed in a full-sized, 8-1/2" x 11" spiral-bound, three-hole-
punched format allowing for easy use and reference.

19 Smart Moves For The Baseball Umpire
19 tips for working a better game — tips you will use no matter what level you
work! Written by Ken Allan, 23-year NCAA Division I baseball umpire. A great
handout for association meetings and officiating camps and clinics! (24-page
booklet) **BSMBA, $2.95, NASO-Member Price: $2.35**

**Association leaders and instructors: Bulk order discounts are available on
all *Referee* officiating books. For details call 414/632-8855 today!**

Qty.	Order code	Description	NASO Price	Price	Amount
	BBUGVI	Baseball Umpires' Guidebook — Volume I	$15.95	$19.95	
	BBUGV2	Baseball Umpires' Guidebook — Volume II	$15.95	$19.95	
	BBUGV3	Baseball Umpires' Guidebook — Volume III	$15.95	$19.95	
	BBUGC	Baseball Umpires' Guidebook — Volumes I, II, III + Binder	$47.95	$59.95	
	BBUGB	Baseball Umpires' Guidebooks Binder	$ 6.35	$ 7.95	
	BSMBA	19 Smart Moves For The Baseball Umpire	$ 2.35	$ 2.95	

Shipping/Handling Chart

Up to $5	$ 2.00
$ 5.01-$ 15	$ 4.00
$ 15.01-$ 30	$ 6.00
$ 30.01-$ 50	$ 8.00
$ 50.01-$ 70	$10.00
$ 70.01-$100	$12.00
$100.01-$250	$15.00
Over $250	CALL FOR RATE

RESIDENTS OUTSIDE 48 CONTIGUOUS STATES: CALL 800/733-6100 FOR SHIPPING RATES.

Subtotal

Wisconsin residents add
5% sales tax

Shipping & Handling
(see chart)

TOTAL

Name_____ Address_____

City, State, Zip_____ Daytime Phone_____

Referee/NASO Account #_____
 ❏ Check/Money order ❏ MasterCard ❏ VISA

Account #_____ Expiration Date_____

Signature_____
(required only if using credit card)

VISA/MasterCard holders
call 800/733-6100
Or 414/632-5448
24-hour service
7 days a week.
Or send check with order to:
REFEREE/NASO Special
Services P.O. Box 12,
Franksville, WI 53126

IF YOU

LIKE THIS

BOOK,

YOU'LL

LOVE

THIS MAGAZINE!

The only magazine exclusively for sports officials

Rulings, caseplays, mechanics – in-depth

Solid coverage of the sport(s) you work

Important, late-breaking news stories

Thought-provoking interviews and features

Opinions/editorials on vital topics

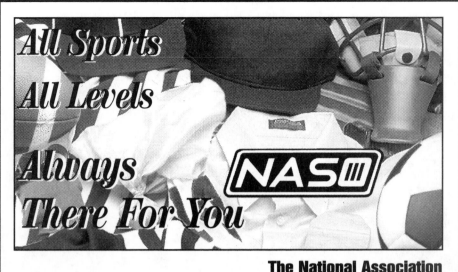
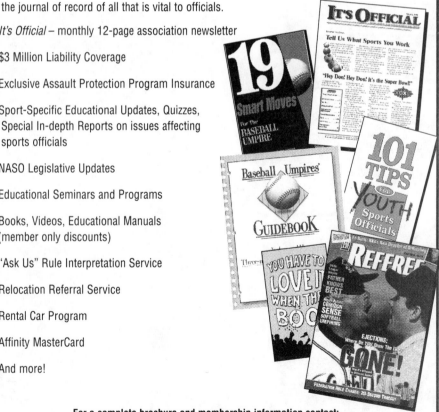